Working with Spirit

*is a Path Book
offering practical spirituality
to enrich everyday living.*

*"Your word is a lamp to my feet
and a light to my path."*
Psalm 119:105

Dedication

For David, my beloved co-worker in parenting and ministry.
And for my colleagues and friends at the University of Guelph.
L.R.

For Susan, whose wisdom and love guide me daily.
And to our daughters, Jerry and Courtney, for their love and support.
F.E.

Gratitudes

I am grateful to those who reviewed parts of this book in its manuscript form and gave their feedback, especially my friends of different faiths – O. P. Dwivedi, Michael Grand, Ken Hood, Bill Hulet, and Iftikhar Sheikh. I also owe a debt of gratitude to the members of the Spirituality in the Workplace groups at the University of Guelph, who have shared their stories, struggles, and joys so honestly and generously, and taught me so much. Special thanks, too, to Robert Maclennan at ABC Publishing for his encouragement as we turned assorted thoughts and stories into this book.
L.R.

First, my thanks to Lucy Reid. When I proposed this book to Lucy, she immediately shared and enhanced my vision. I am also grateful to Lucy for keeping our writing moving along when there were many other tasks vying for our attention. Lucy truly represents spirit at work at the University of Guelph.

I too am grateful for the guidance we received on this book from our colleagues at the University of Guelph and from Robert Maclennan at ABC Publishing. I would also like to acknowledge Margaret Murray and John Veltri, SJ, for helping me understand spirituality at work issues.
F.E.

December 2003

Working with Spirit

Engaging Spirituality to Meet the Challenges of the Workplace

Lucy Reid & Fred Evers

Path Books
A LIGHT TO MY PATH

Path Books, Anglican Book Centre
General Synod of the Anglican Church of Canada
80 Hayden Street, Toronto, Ontario, Canada M4Y 3G2
abcpublishing@national.anglican.ca
www.abcpublishing.com www.pathbooks.com

Biblical quotations are from the New Revised Standard Version, Thomas Nelson Publishers: Nashville, 1989. Adapted slightly by the authors occasionally.

Text set in Daily News Regular
Cover and text design by Jane Thornton
Cover photograph by Jane Thornton

Library and Archives of Canada Cataloguing in Publication

Reid, Lucy
    Working with spirit: engaging spirituality to meet the challenges of the workplace / Lucy Reid and Fred Evers.

ISBN 1-55126-417-X

1. Work. 2. Spirituality. 3. Work — Religious aspects — Christianity.
4. Spirituality — Christianity. I. Evers, Frederick T. (Frederick Thomas),
1949– II. Title.

BL65.W67R43 2004   248.8'8   C2004-903272-0

Contents

Spirituality and Work

We live in interesting times. In Canada, as elsewhere in North America and Europe, our society is generally considered to be secular, with religion and state separate and the overt role of religion in public life minimal. Over the last fifty years there has been a massive decline in church membership and religious practice. In Canada in 1957, for example, according to statistics gathered by sociologist of religion Reginald Bibby in *Restless Gods* [2002], 53% of all Canadians were attending religious services weekly. By the year 2000 that figure had plummeted to 24%. Among Canadian teens, in 2000 one in four was identified as having no religion at all [Bibby 2002, 20, 86]. Even allowing for a rejection of religion that is temporary and age-related, the phenomenon of spiritually disenfranchised youth and young adults is new and challenging.

Paradoxically, at the same time as this shift away from organized religion, interest in spirituality is greater than ever. People are searching. According to Bibby, they are not dropping out of religion altogether so much as dropping in — church-shopping, testing the waters, looking for meaning and guidance without committing to regular membership and practice. They are responding to an inner voice that drives them to ask questions and seek answers in a variety of places and in a variety of ways.

The commercial response to this quest is a growing number of books, retreat centres, conferences, and leaders in the field of spirituality. The mainline churches may be struggling with membership decline, but the shelves of any bookstore are well stocked with titles on spirituality of all kinds. It is as though the new religion is spirituality: "I'm not religious, but I am spiritual" is today's creed. As spirituality has widened beyond the container of organized religion, people have been exploring and experimenting for themselves, and looking for ways to relate spirituality to the whole of life. In particular, the notion of a spirituality of work is emerging. Books, speakers, even web sites are focusing for the first time on spirituality in the workplace.

What is meant by this phrase? There is a recognition that as human beings we have spiritual needs and drives as well as physical, mental, emotional, and social ones. We do not leave our soul at the door of the workplace. It enters with us and can either help us engage more deeply, meaningfully, and compassionately with our work, or reveal to us the futility, ferocity, or soul-destroying aspects of work. As poet and author David Whyte writes in *The Heart Aroused: Poetry and the Preservation of Soul in Corporate America*, "If work is all about *doing*, then the soul is all about *being*.... [We are exploring] the possibility of being at home in the world, melding soul life with work life, the inner ocean of longing and belonging with the outer ground of strategy and organizational control" [Whyte 1994, 201].

The spirit within us needs purpose and meaning as much as the body needs food and water. The context of the workplace, in which we spend so many of our waking hours, raises profoundly spiritual questions, if we choose to hear them, such as:

Is this all there is?

What would I be doing if I didn't have to earn a living?

Is my work worthwhile? Does it benefit the world in some way?

Am I what I do, or is there more?

Where is God in my work?

On my death bed will I look back and be glad I did this?

Each of these questions addresses something deeper than the surface issues of productivity, employability, income level, seniority, and so on. These are the questions that float up and catch us unawares in unguarded or vulnerable moments. They can accuse and confuse. No one has prepared us for these, in the way we learned how to write exams and résumés, manage interviews and people. Our workplace throws these questions at us, but supplies no answers. Even discussion of such matters is rare and uncomfortable at work, and we risk being seen as religious fanatics when we raise them. Yet the questions remain, and they have a way of haunting us and tripping us if we try to ignore them, sending us physical and emotional symptoms such as headaches, insomnia, irritability, restlessness.

When we dare to ask ourselves, "Why am I spending my life's energy in this way?" we are setting foot on a path that can open the heart to a renewed sense of vocation and purpose, and a deepened understanding of life. This path leads us to God, to the Spirit beyond and behind and within our spirits. And so the workplace need not be the enemy of our spirituality, but the crucible in which our spiritual life is burnished and shaped.

Spirituality in the workplace, then, is not a cunning managerial strategy to make us more docile drones, nor is it a token nod in the direction of God at work, like saying the Lord's Prayer at school. It is the pursuit of meaning and integrity, the attentiveness to deep questions, the unleashing of creativity, by which our work is humanized and sanctified. This book is oriented to the spiritual explorers of today who seek understanding of how their work relates to their spirituality. Spiritual explorers seek a richer life for themselves, their families, and their colleagues at work. They want work that goes beyond a pay cheque and rungs on the corporate ladder. They search for a higher purpose to their work and lives. They search for a way to handle life's hardships: the death of a colleague, a sick child, divorce, job loss.

For many of us, most of the time, our work feels anything but sacred. Where the rubber hits the road, there are skid marks more often than smooth acceleration to God. As we were working on this book, for example, we became distracted and bogged down by the demands of full-time work, the ups and downs of family life, problems at our churches, personal health issues, and sickness and tragedy among friends – in short, the tangled stuff of life. We wanted to write about finding God at work, but were in danger of blatant hypocrisy as we struggled unsuccessfully to balance our own lives and live by our spiritual beliefs.

We are not experts, then, so much as people who care enough about the questions to ask them aloud and embark on the journey toward answers. We are all too aware of the problems and pains of the workplace in this twenty-first century world. We know that work is stressful and hard, whether it is digging up roads, designing software, or caring for children. We take seriously statistics such as the decline in job satisfaction among Canadians, from 62% in 1991 to 45% in 2001, as related by Tom Harpur in *Finding the Still Point: A Spiritual Response to Stress* [2002, 11]. Canadian researcher Linda Duxbury reports that absenteeism in the Canadian workforce costs some $3 billion (Canadian) per year. [See her survey report *Voices of Canadians*, published in 2003.]

The workplace in our culture has become almost synonymous with stress, overwork, instability, and flux. Duxbury's research shows that 25% of Canadians are working more than fifty hours a week, compared to only 10% doing so ten years ago; 30% report depression; 40% cannot face going into work some days and take "mental health" days off, and an alarming 60% report feeling high levels of stress from work. Reginald Bibby's research has found that 48% of Canadians polled in 2000 said that their top personal concern was seeming never to have enough time [Bibby, 2002, 205]. People are feeling stretched to the limit, with very little downtime for recovery and few spiritual resources to sustain them.

We are writing as two people engaged in a modern workplace with all its problems. This is not an academic analysis or a theological work, but a book for all spiritual explorers, regardless of their religious background, who are trying to integrate spirit and soul with work and daily life. We are both Christians, and clearly our faith influences the way we think and write. If we were Jewish or Muslim, this book would be different, but we hope that all readers will find it useful.

The perspectives we bring are broadly sociological and theological. Between us we have expertise in teaching, working with organizations, preparing students for the work world, and addressing the spiritual needs of people at various life stages. As a sociologist and a priest we have different working lives, but a shared desire to find God, spirit, holiness in the ordinary world, and to live connected to that sustaining centre. We do not have the answers to all the challenges of the workplace. Life, as Scott Peck memorably wrote, is difficult. And work will always be challenging. But we do have some insights into the simple gifts and truths that lie at the heart of spirituality, and we are convinced that as these are engaged so our work will be leavened and sanctified.

The book is structured in a straightforward way. *Part One: The Challenges of the Workplace* deals with issues of work today on three levels — the personal, the corporate, and the societal. Chapter 1 focuses on *individuals* dealing with the fragmentation between public and spiritual life. We look at the way life became compartmentalized over the centuries, and spirituality became divorced from work. Where God and prayer were a central part of agrarian living, the impersonal factories were soulless and seemed far removed from what was sacred. The legacy for individuals today is a disconnection between the public persona at work in the world, and the private being whose beliefs, longings and joys are kept locked out of sight and out of play during working hours.

Chapter 2 deals with the *workplace*. It looks at the reasons we work, and the way that we tend to define ourselves by our work, and then fall prey to its destructive characteristics of overwork, conflict, anxiety, and burnout. Chapter 3 is oriented to issues at a *cultural* level, and considers how competition, consumerism, and materialism, the cornerstones of our economy, contribute to an unsustainable situation for both individuals and organizations, leading to collapse. Throughout these chapters and the three subsequent ones, which parallel them, we seed the text with stories of real and fictional people who are grappling with the issues we raise, and we pose questions for individual reflection or group discussion. We hope that this brings life and relevance to the topics we present.

Part Two: Simple Gifts presents ways to heal the fragmentation [chapter 4], humanize the workplace [chapter 5], and embrace virtues that run counter to the culture's norms [chapter 6], by engaging the spiritual truths that have always been known and taught, but so often forgotten or neglected. We look at the concept of vocation, for example, as an alternative to the worldly wisdom that a job is just a means of making money. The Sabbath tradition is discussed, with its gift of bringing balance and rest to the week. And the simple but radical gifts of community, simplicity, and freedom are reaffirmed as crucial, if our frantic work world is to be made saner and healthier.

Chapter 7 looks specifically at the Christian contribution to our understanding of spirituality in the workplace, through a selection of sayings of Jesus and writings of Christians. In chapter 8, acknowledging the reality that we live in a multi-faith world, and grateful for what we are learning from non-Christian traditions, we touch on some of the wisdom from other world religions, as it pertains to work. The book concludes with a compendium of resources in chapter 9 and a list of suggested reading in chapter 10, aimed at providing practical ways for people to start on this journey of engaging spirituality to meet the challenges of the workplace.

PART ONE

The Challenges
of the Workplace

--- CHAPTER 1 ---

A Fragmented Life

In order to understand what spirituality in the workplace can offer, we need to reflect on the evolution of work. A workplace characterized by a relatively "flat" hierarchy, career switches, multi-tasking, email, and a thirst for spirituality is a new phenomenon. We need to consider how we arrived at this point in our history. We will focus on three stages of the evolution of Western society: agrarian society, industrial society, and today's post-modern society.

Agrarian society

In the nineteenth century Canada was primarily an agrarian society. There were hunters and fishers, carpenters, crafts people, government workers, merchants, ministers, police, and teachers, but most people worked at home and farmed. Many societies in the world evolved from an agrarian base, and of course, in many parts of the world there are still societies that are agrarian.

What was life like in an agrarian society? There was a strong sense of community and a reliance on family. Families tended to be larger than today, with sons and daughters working on the farm as soon as they were able. In an agrarian society many needs had to be met by families and the immediate community. Home schooling was common (and we still see examples of home schooling in rural communities today). Farmers raised a variety of crops and livestock to meet the family's needs as well as to sell. Worship was a communal activity. Life still revolved around the farm. Boys and girls would have to miss school when they were needed at home to help with the harvest. An interesting note is that some school districts in Canada today continue to delay the start of classes when necessary, to accommodate the harvest.

Agrarian life centred on farming and the seasons: spring planting, summer weeding, fall harvest, and winter maintenance. Spirituality was tied to the land and weather. Fields were blessed before they were seeded. Farmers prayed for rain, warm temperatures, and a late frost. When the harvest was safely in, the community would gather in the church to give thanks, and then celebrate together with a harvest supper. Life, work, and spirituality were interconnected and reinforced each other. Life and work were not separated — there was no need to go home after work, because work was done at home.

In an agrarian society life for everyone revolved around farming. Merchants did not make many sales when crops were poor. Teachers lost their students to farming at harvest and other times when their labour was needed. The whole community was affected by bad weather or crop failure. Even those not actively involved in producing food from the land were directly dependent upon it in very immediate ways.

It is easy to think nostalgically about a slower paced way of life based on community and family. It can seem idyllic in contrast to today's hurried and impersonal lifestyle. But there were many hardships and difficulties as well. Farming required arduous work with very long hours and uncertain outcomes. And no matter how hard a family worked, the crop could be ruined by a hailstorm, flood, or drought. But for many generations farming was the mainstay of life and work in Canada.

Although farming has continued to be an important part of the Canadian economy, Statistics Canada reports that currently only 330,000 Canadians are employed in agriculture, or 2.1% of all those employed. The size of farms continues to increase from an average of 207 hectares per farm in 1981 to 273 hectares in 2001. Many contemporary farms are now huge agribusiness organizations run by managers who do not necessarily own or live on the farms they manage. Far fewer families plough today, and the farms they work have increased in size and production. While agriculture provides food both for domestic use and for export, and many agricultural communities are still tied to a strong sense of community, Canadian society is no longer an agrarian one.

Family snapshot, 1803: John and Eliza

What was life like in 1803 for an average family? John and Eliza (fictitious) settled in Upper Canada (now Ontario) along Lake Ontario. They had a large family of eight children, and John's brother, Matthew, lived with them. One child died soon after he was born in 1794. John, Matthew, and the older children all worked on their farm. They grew a variety of vegetables for themselves and several hectares of wheat to sell. They had a horse that was used to pull the plough and their wagon when the family went to town. John had been able to buy two cows after last year's harvest, so they now had a supply of milk. Eliza maintained the household. She cared for the children, cooked all the meals, made butter and soap, and cleaned the family's clothes.

The town's first church was going to be built after this year's harvest, if the harvest proved to be a good one. In the meantime, they worshipped each Sunday at a neighbour's house. They were also anxious for a school to be built, but it was decided that the church would be built first and it could be used as a school for the younger children during the week. In the evenings Eliza was teaching each of her children to read and write. John was illiterate, but he understood the importance of reading and writing and marvelled at Eliza's ability to teach the children.

John felt tied to the land they now farmed. It had been a struggle to settle in this area, build a house and barn and clear the land, but he loved the farm and the work. John was deeply spiritual — he prayed each morning and led the prayers at suppertime. He often asked Eliza to read passages of the

Bible to him after the children went to bed. Matthew was not as keen on the Bible as John, but he did enjoy listening to Eliza read. John and Eliza found the strength to deal with hardships through their belief in God.

Industrial society

Where did all the farmers go? The simple answer is that they went to the growing cities during and after the industrial revolution. They were attracted by factory jobs with fixed hours. Some left because of problems on their farms. There were many reasons, but one outcome — a decline in the characteristics of an agrarian society and an increase in a new way of life where needs were met outside of the family. Work, health care, education, protection, worship, and other societal needs were all centralized in various organizations: factories, hospitals, schools, police forces, and churches. Family was still very important (as it is today), but the linkages between work and family, spirituality and family, and work and spirituality began to break down.

Spirituality without its linkages to the land and to work became much more formalized. Religions, as the purveyors of spirituality, grew. Churches, synagogues, and temples were built throughout the cities. Houses of worship grew in numbers and functions. Community events, adult religious teaching, Sunday school, meetings, and other activities were held in churches, synagogues, and temples. These buildings became central to the community. Many of today's church buildings, for example, were built in the late 1800s and early 1900s, during the population expansion and urbanization that Canada experienced.

In a more diverse society with people engaged in many different types of work the interconnections that existed in an agrarian society were lost in the industrial age. Perhaps the greatest change in the industrial period was the split between work and family life. In an agrarian society, the two were linked — we still refer to the "family farm." Farming was a family matter. In the industrial age, the father went off to work, the mother looked after the children and the house, and the children went to school. A separation of roles was created, and a compartmentalizing of life developed.

Work in a factory was not dependent on the land or the weather. The cycle of the seasons did not have a direct impact on most forms of industrial work. And for most workers, every day was the same repetition of a very specific task thousands of times. The industrial age created a great diversity of jobs, and the rise of unions eventually helped to ensure fair wages, safety, and reasonable hours. But the work was often boring, the workers were disconnected from their roots, and social upheaval was common.

Family snapshot, 1903: Jack and Bessie

Jack and Bessie had lived on farms all their lives. When they married, they thought that they would take over Jack's father's farm. But their lives went in a different direction when Jack's father died and Jack learned that the farm had to be sold to pay off debts that had built up over the last ten years due to poor crops. They considered living at the farm owned by Bessie's family, but there were several older brothers in line to inherit the farm. So, they decided to go to Toronto and look for work and a place to live. Jack found a job in a new factory that made stoves. When he started work, the owner had set things up so that a group of men built a complete stove from the parts made at a foundry. The work was hard and dirty, but Jack liked his fellow workers and was pleased to see the finished stove. However, after a trip to Ford's plant in Detroit, the factory's owner decided to convert to a Ford-type assembly line. Now each worker did one task over and over. The number of stoves produced increased greatly, and the owner was able to pay the workers more. Jack appreciated the extra money, but he hated the monotonous work.

Bessie spent her time at home in their small house on the outskirts of town. She cleaned and cared for their four children. When they were old enough, the children went to school. As they grew up, Bessie found being at home more and more lonely during the day. She missed the country. But Bessie and Jack were strong people and did not show their frustrations to each other. The family went to church every Sunday, and gradually Jack and Bessie became involved in church projects. Jack became a church warden and felt that he regained some of the pride he had lost at the assembly line, where a manager watched his every move.

Post-modern society

While there are still many elements of an agrarian society and an industrial society in Canada today, we have moved into a new era. What it will finally be called is hard to say. It is characterized by changes in the labour force, in work, and in organizational structures; by the use of information technology; by new ethical issues; and by individualism, fragmentation, and a search for spirituality. We want to explore what some of these changes and developments mean for the workplace today.

The Canadian population and the labour force have become more diverse with every generation. The labour force is made up of men and women from many cultural backgrounds, bringing a vast range of skills and values to the organizations that employ them. And Canadians bring a wide range of spiritual beliefs to the workplace, although mostly invisibly and silently.

Most Canadians work in the service industries now: tourism, education, and government. Large industry is still present, notably the automobile industry, but the trend is toward small and medium sized organizations. Individuals are likely to have more than one career in their lifetime, not just multiple jobs. One projection is that the average will be four or five different careers. The rise and fall of "dot-com" businesses operating through the Internet has shown us just how quickly major trends can change in today's society.

The current stage in societal development has been called "post-modernism." Although it defies any exact definition, one of the characteristics of post-modernism is extreme fluidity, with a preference for diversity over uniformity, fragmentation over cohesion, individualism over communalism, and ambivalence or open-endedness over certainty. Everything is perceived to be in a state of flux. Change and uncertainty are the new normal. The individual must decide what is right for him or herself, and there is no longer automatic respect for institutions of governance and authority.

The workplace in a post-modern society poses new challenges. It is unpredictable — careers can soar or crash with very little warning. It is demanding — the number of hours spent at work is increasing, despite the earlier projections that this would be a leisured generation. It is dislocated — many people drive significant distances to work, or work from home at computers, miles or even provinces away from the organization that employs them. And the post-modern workplace is secular: faith has no place in it, and the question of religious belief or practice is passed over in silence or embarrassment.

Family snapshot, 2003: Johnny and Liz

Johnny and Liz live in a spacious executive home north of Toronto. Liz is a systems programmer and Johnny is a corporate lawyer. They both work downtown and love the fast pace of Toronto. They have thought about having children, but Liz has decided to wait until she is at a point in her career when she can take some time off. Johnny agrees with this, but worries that they will wait too long. Their parents on both sides went to church, but Johnny and Liz do not see the relevance and would hate to give up their Sunday mornings — about the only time that they have for themselves.

Recently Liz went through a difficult period. The information technology company that she worked for had downsized, and her division was sold to another company. She declined a position offered by the new company because it was at a lower salary than her previous job. Liz felt that she would have no trouble finding another position. Unfortunately she entered the labour market at a bad time and could not find a job consistent with her experience and skills. Johnny was very supportive but, like Liz, he started to worry about being able to handle their huge mortgage payments if Liz could not find work soon.

As the days went by Liz felt more and more discouraged. Johnny and her parents were kind and told her that she would soon find a job. But she felt panic-stricken and alone, with no anchor to hold onto. Without the income she was used to, she began to wonder if her life was worthwhile at all. Like Johnny, Liz has no religious affiliation. She describes herself sometimes as "spiritual," but she has never explored what this might mean.

From integration to fragmentation

Societal trends from agrarian to industrial to post-modern can be characterized as moving from integration to separation and fragmentation, and from communal to individualistic. Spirituality and religion are now strictly private and personal matters, not societal or even family ones. Many couples raise their children with no religious beliefs or practices, either because it seems to have no relevance to life, or in the hope that they will choose a spiritual path for themselves as adults. The idea of a family worshipping together and handing on a tradition has been widely rejected. According to Statistics Canada, before 1971 only 1% of the Canadian adult population identified themselves as having no religion. By 2001, in certain provinces the number had climbed to as high as 37%, and a total of 16% of Canadians overall reported that they had no religion.

At the same time, the different aspects of being human — emotional, physical, mental, social, spiritual — are treated as separate categories. We have a vast variety of places to go for all the parts of ourselves to be taken care of: a therapist, a chiropractor, a medical doctor, a book club, a service club, a church, a meditation centre, a Tai Chi class. Each is usually quite independent of the others. So the workplace is seen as just one more place, to which we bring certain parts of ourselves. No wonder the neighbourhoods we live in often consist of strangers living side by side. We may have no idea at all what the person across the street does for a living, or believes in, or wrestles with. As our society has become more fragmented, so it has become more anonymous.

The result can be a feeling of dislocation and disorientation: where do I belong, and who am I anyway? Am I the person who drives to work and relates efficiently and effectively with those in my field, or am I the spouse and parent who has difficult teenage children, ageing relatives, and a bad back? Which role is the real me? Do they have any point of overlap, or are they different worlds? And what do I do when they spill over into each other?

In the workplace we can create the self-image that we

choose: our colleagues or clients rarely know anything about our private lives. But there can be a terrible loss in this — loss of depth, loss of integration, loss of reality. Our work in the world can be out of step with our inner life and longings. It may pay the bills, but at the same time it can cause depression or frustration if our soul is not engaged. It is as though we are leaving part of ourselves at the door when we walk into work.

~ ~ ~

Fred's story

There are two sides to my work. I am a spouse, father, teacher, researcher, writer, and professor of sociology. As a professor for many years I was quite reserved and formal at the university. Although I love to teach and do research, I didn't often show my true feelings at work. And, although I felt fulfilled in my work, there was another calling that I finally heard. It came from a friend who works for the diocese. She invited me to be on staff for the Niagara Youth Conference. My co-workers (both young and old) didn't know me as a professor; they knew me as a friend, youth worker, and "enthusiastic" guitar player. In this work I was not reserved. I discovered that I loved organizing and working at youth events and playing my twelve-string guitar. I was accepted as a leader with skills — not because I have a PhD or have worked at universities for a long time. In fact, no one even wanted to see my résumé! I was accepted because I genuinely loved the work. I truly enjoyed the seamless connection of working at youth events and spirituality. I experienced a strong sense of spirituality doing this work. I also started journaling, presenting journaling workshops, and playing the guitar at Taizé services as a result of my work with youth groups.

Many years have passed since I started working with youth, and when I reflect on the experience I realize that, to a certain degree, my work as a professor has merged with my youth work. I try to bring the fun and spirituality of youth events to my daily work. I try to bring the spontaneity and openness of youth to my work as a professor. Every once in a while when I'm walking on campus, I hear, "Hey, Fred!" from one of the youth who knew me as Fred the Youth Worker and has become a University of Guelph student. These reunions typically involve a long conversation about how things are going and end with a hug. And Fred the Professor thinks that's great.

Self-identity

Our self-identity is now a matter of choice. And we have more choices than ever before. In agrarian society people's identity was largely predetermined, and based on the family and community. You were Robert Smith's son. You would be expected to help your father run the farm and someday take it over. In industrial society identity was found in work. You were a miner and part of a fraternity of those doing the same work. Or you were a factory worker and union member. Today identity is an individually constructed matter. You are a computer programmer. Whether or not you have a family is a side issue. Your parents' work is irrelevant. Your company cannot claim your loyalty or sense of belonging, because you may leave any time you choose and even start a completely different line of work. And your religious or spiritual beliefs are your own. No one is likely to ask you about them at work. You can choose to be a member of a church or not — there is very little social pressure; in fact there is probably more pressure not to go. You may choose to search for a spirituality that fits your sense of self.

The point of this book is not to bemoan the decline of organized religion in Canada. The point is to try to offer the reader an understanding of spirituality that can be integrated into life and work, so that a sense of God can develop *in the midst of* daily activities. This in turn can heal some of the fragmentation we live with, and root our core identity on something solid and dependable. The spirit or soul has classically been understood as residing deep inside, where the real "me" is, beyond the projections and pretenses and problems of our lives. In this ever-changing world we badly need to rediscover the soul in order to anchor our lives on a firm, integrating foundation.

Questions

What are the different compartments of your life?

How porous are the walls between them? For example, many of us bring some of our work home. How often do you bring part of your home life to work, and how does that feel?

Is spirituality a part of your work?

--- CHAPTER 2 ---
Workplace Woes

Why do we work?

This may sound like a silly question. There is a sense of necessity about work: it is just something we have to do. We need to earn money to buy groceries, pay off the mortgage or pay rent, pay for our children's orthodontic needs, hockey gear, and on and on. Our ancestors had to work to stay alive, literally. If they did not hunt, fish, and grow enough food in the summer, they would starve in the winter.

Farmers understand this sort of work. They do what they need to do each day. For some days this means working long hours to bring in a crop before the rain or frost. Other days there is time to chat with neighbours over the fence. Farmers work with nature — they know that they cannot ignore the weather. Some things cannot be done in the rain so another task is quickly chosen — there is always lots to do.

For most of us, our work is not dependent on nature the way it is for farmers. Most of us do the same work whether it rains or shines. We don't need to look to the sky to decide what to do each day, although we may need to shovel snow from our driveways in order to get to work. Yet working in an office often feels as much a necessity as toiling in a field. We are still working for our survival, though in a more abstract way than our great-grandparents or our agricultural neighbours. We are working to stay afloat, get ahead, be secure. The thought of being without an income terrifies us as much as the prospect of being without food or shelter terrified our forebears. Work provides us with much that we consider essential.

But at a deeper level work offers far more than mere survival. If it were just a matter of making money, we would all compete for the same jobs — the ones that pay the best. But we have a society with thousands of different jobs, some paying well and some paying poorly. People seek work that interests them and fits with who they are, because work is a fundamental part of our identity. We gain satisfaction from our work, not just an income. We experience a sense of contributing to society through our work. Many people pursue higher education because it will help them find jobs that are challenging and that mesh well with their sense of identity. Precisely because work is so highly valued, societally and personally, those without work can feel excluded and discounted.

Psychologist Abraham Maslow (1908–1970) referred to a hierarchy of needs that human beings experience, starting with physical needs and going through to the need for self-actualization. Our most basic needs, he said, are for things such as food, water, and safety. We then look for "higher" needs to be fulfilled, such as the need for relationship or belonging, and the need for self-esteem and feelings of worth.

Lastly, if these previous needs are met, we seek self-actualization, or a sense of personal fulfilment of our potential. And if that occurs we experience what Maslow called "peak experiences" — deep moments of happiness, love, and understanding; feelings of being intensely alive; a passionate concern for justice and harmony.

Maslow wrote in his classic work *Motivation and Personality*, "Musicians must make music, artists must paint, poets must write if they are to be ultimately at peace with themselves. What humans *can* be, they *must* be" [Maslow 1987, 22, original emphases]. His studies of the workings of the human mind led him to believe that for optimum mental health and wellbeing, a person's potential had to be tapped. It is not enough simply to feed, clothe, and occupy human beings. Work, therefore, may provide us with the necessities of life, but it can also meet some of our deepest or highest needs, as we reach for our vocation, personal fulfilment, and a sense of peace with ourselves and the world.

———

Questions

What are your reasons for working?

Which of your needs are being met through your work?

Which are not being met?

Defined by our work

Even those of us lucky enough to have well-paying and fulfilling work have problems keeping it in its place. Work may provide us with the necessities of life and a sense of satisfaction and fulfilment, but it can also take over our lives. And perhaps the problem that besets our work more than anything else is our over-identification with it. We define ourselves by the work we do, and thus give it primacy in our lives.

Consider the way we typically introduce ourselves to each other in social settings: "I'm Lucy. I'm a chaplain at the University of Guelph." … "I'm Fred. I'm a professor of sociology." It is the language of employment and occupation. Only very unusually would we introduce ourselves by referring instead, for example, to our key relationships: "I'm Lucy. I'm married to David and we have three teenage children." … "I'm Fred. My wife is Susan and we have two wonderful adult daughters." Similarly, the question, "What do you do?" is often answered with a response not about *doing* but about *being*: "I am a teacher." A teacher becomes who I am, not just a job I do. My work defines me. So I evaluate myself according to that definition, I build or lose my self-esteem in the workplace, and I wonder who I am when the role ends with retirement or redundancy.

Naturally there is a tremendous amount of anxiety around getting and keeping a job, not only because work is the main source of income for most people, but also because of the identity issue. Parents exert pressure on their children to get a job, to "be somebody!" It is as though, without work, we are nobodies. And so work can easily become tyrannical in its emotional — even existential — hold over us.

One of the themes of the popular British movie *The Full Monty* is the breakdown of male identity in a situation of widespread unemployment. One character, formerly a manager, has been going out every day, apparently to work as usual, but hiding from his wife the fact that he, too, has been made redundant. Without his job he considers himself to be a nobody, ashamed, so all he can do is pretend. Stories abound also of those who gave their all to their jobs and then died shortly after retirement, as though the body did not know what to do without work to go to and focus on; or workers who were made redundant and went crazy, bursting into their former workplace armed and ready to kill. Work, then, can meet our material needs and fulfil our need for meaningful self-expression and development, but when it becomes the primary lens through which we see the world and ourselves, it can be a ruthless captor.

Workaholism

Slavery was abolished more than one hundred years ago, but a subtler form of imprisonment has emerged in the modern workplace, which we know as workaholism. Author and poet David Whyte, in his book *Crossing the Unknown Sea*, refers to this as a post-modern form of serfdom, where there is a crippling lack of time and spaciousness in our working lives, because of our entanglement in a culture that demands an endless cycle of production and consuming [Whyte 2001, 164].

Like an alcoholic, the workaholic is trapped in a pattern of destructive behaviour over which he or she feels there is little or no control. Long hours at work are the norm, with "time management" techniques being used to shoe horn as much as possible into the working day. The pace and stress level of work escalate to the breaking point. The "rock bottom" that the workaholic hits is complete burnout, with physical, mental, emotional, spiritual, and social collapse. Typically family life breaks down first, as the workaholic spends more and more hours either at work or consumed by work worries, and withdraws from family activities. There may be initial rewards for this — a bigger pay cheque, promotion, the boss's approval. In fact, it has been said that workaholism is the only addiction that is socially sanctioned and rewarded: getting ahead by working around the clock and sacrificing one's personal life is often held up as an admirable path. The toll is brushed under the carpet.

Of course, there have periodically been times in human history when groups of people have had to work very arduously, from the European immigrants who settled in this country to today's emergency workers at disaster sites. But it is a new phenomenon for people in modern society in normal circumstances to be choosing, seemingly, to overwork. In post-World War II Japan, during its technological boom, workaholism became almost a cultural norm, and a new word, *karoshi* (meaning "death by overwork"), entered Japanese vocabulary, as the up and coming executives, and sometimes even students, worked themselves into the grave or committed suicide on failing to accomplish their goals.

Sam's story

*Sam is an executive in a thriving company. He holds
an MBA and rose rapidly to his vice-president position.
His large salary enables him to own a fine house as
well as a cottage, and to take expensive vacations with
his wife and family. The only problem is that, for the
last four years, Sam has not taken more than a couple
of days' vacation time in a row. He is just too busy.
Even when he does take some time off, he keeps his cell
phone with him, and his palm pilot, and his laptop
computer, so that he can respond to the urgent and
incessant demands of the office.*

*Sam's family has become accustomed to holidaying
without him, and he tells himself that this is for the best.
He's poised on one of the top rungs of the ladder, and
to become CEO and the best provider he can be, he
knows he must make sacrifices.*

*But Sam is lonely. Sometimes when he gets home
late from work, his wife and children are already asleep
in bed. He often sits alone in the darkened house
drinking a nightcap so that he can unwind and feel
better. And he secretly dreams of one day walking
away from the world he knows and starting a new life.
But until then, he feels as though the high-rise office
building where he works is his prison.*

Burnout

Many of us at work today would admit to fitting the "HALT" definition of burnout: we are hungry, angry, lonely, and tired. We are over-eating (or over-drinking) to comfort ourselves, lashing out at colleagues or family members when the elastic of being over-stretched snaps, feeling isolated and alone as we toil ever harder, and suffering from constant fatigue. As noted ealier, sociologist Reginald Bibby asked Canadians what concerned them most in life, and 48% identified not having enough time as their number one problem [Bibby 2002, 205]. Worse still, there seems to be no way out. We feel trapped. The very jobs that promised to provide for us and give our lives meaning have us in a stranglehold, because if I am what I do, then ceasing to do threatens the core of my existence. Far from providing our livelihood, work sometimes threatens to squeeze the life right out of us and leave us limp and exhausted rags.

Many employers expect their employees to do what it takes to get the job done. If this means working one hundred-hour weeks, then fine. If it means missing your daughter's piano recital, never mind — there will be other recitals. These expectations are usually not written down anywhere, but new employees quickly learn what it takes to keep their job and advance in the organization. They comply, but often harbour deep resentment. Yet when their turn comes to set expectations and standards, they will often demand the same of others, arguing that if they themselves have had to do this, there's no reason why others can't. And so our work patterns are perpetuated, and the singe of burnout hovers almost visibly in the air.

It may be that reining in the insatiable demands of work and keeping it from absorbing all our energy is one of the quintessential challenges of our time. A spirituality for the workplace must engage with this challenge and help us find the wisdom and courage to do things differently, swimming against the tide of a work-addicted culture. With a perspective that values each one as a person, regardless of income or career standing, we can detach our self-worth from our work just a little, and become freer to step back from the proverbial rat race.

～～～

Questions

How many hours a week are you working?

Why?

Downsizing and under-utilization

In the last two decades, in Canada and elsewhere, significant changes in the workplace have occurred, placing new stressors on workers. Some organizations have downsized, no longer employing as many people. Some of the changes have been structural; for example, many large organizations have reduced the number of "levels" between the top position (chief executive officer or president) and the bottom position. In large bureaucratic organizations such as a government agency the structures traditionally resembled a steep pyramid, with many levels of managers, department heads, and vice-presidents between the top and the bottom. By reducing the number of levels from, say, ten or more to three or four, the organization is reducing the number of workers and changes the structure of the organization and the way work is done there. (It is important to note that often the "middle level" positions that are dropped by many organizations are advanced level, managerial positions.)

Let's pause for a moment and consider a question. If an organization drops several levels or layers of managers, what happens to the people who keep their jobs?

Many of them are going to have to do more work — their pre-change work plus the work of other staff who lost their jobs. And many workers will not only have to do more work; they will have to be able to work with less supervision. They will have to make more decisions on their own, take on more responsibility. This isn't all bad. Some workers will relish the added responsibility. Some will thrive in the new workplace. But without a doubt, most employees in today's organizations are finding themselves doing more work and suffering from increased stress and fatigue as a result.

At the same time, under-utilization is a serious problem. It includes unemployment, part-time employment (where full-time is desired), and under-employment. Human knowledge, skills, and imagination — gifts from God — are squandered by under-utilization all too often. Where over-work causes burn-out, under-work causes rust-out.

There was a series of advertisements on TV some years ago to encourage giving money to African-American colleges in the US. Each ad was a vignette about an African-American student who might not be able to go to college. The ads ended with the slogan, "A mind is a terrible thing to waste." This quotation captures the under-utilization of workers.

The rate of unemployment changes somewhat from year to year, and it varies across regions in Canada, but whatever the rate is, it represents real people who often feel neglected and without value. Since we define each other in terms of what we "do," people who are unemployed may feel that they do not have an identity. As we experience an ever in-creasing rate of technological change that continuously alters the workplace, more and more people are likely to experi-ence periods of unemployment. There is dignity in work, and being without work can rob us of our dignity and sense of purpose. "A mind is a terrible thing to waste." We need to be equipped to cope with unemployment (expected or unex-pected) and *not* let a period of unemployment define us.

Part-time employment is another form of under-utiliza-tion. There are many situations where people desire part-time work and request it from employers, for example, a parent who needs to be home half-days with a child in kindergarten. Another example would be a person who is self-employed but needs to supplement that income with part-time work. The under-utilization aspect occurs when individuals are *forced* to settle for part-time employment. Many settle for several part-time jobs. Often university students find themselves in this situation. Part-time positions create flexibility for employers, and since part-time or occasional workers typically do not have contracts, they can be fired (and hired back) easily. Part-time workers also do not typically qualify for employee benefits. In essence they become expendable and cheapened. "A mind is a terrible thing to waste."

Under-employment is in some ways the worst form of under-utilization of workers. Under-employment is hiring people to fill positions that do not require their knowledge and skills. The taxi driver with a PhD is the example that journalists love to describe. The reality is that under-employment is widespread and a true waste of our precious human resource. Sociologists who have studied this inconsistency between job requirements and employees' credentials argue that employers need to increase the complexity of work that, say, college graduates occupy. An economist might argue that the problem is really "over-education" and society should produce fewer college graduates if there are not enough jobs that require college degrees. Regardless of one's perspective on the origin of the problem, it is evident that people need to find jobs that are consistent with their education, knowledge, and skills. Being over-qualified for the work individuals are doing can be very discouraging, especially when the long-term prospects are not positive. "A mind is a terrible thing to waste."

Under-utilization has to be addressed from two viewpoints. At the macro level, how can we — through our governments — encourage and support employers and entrepreneurs to create more jobs and jobs that use the knowledge, skills, and imaginations of all our people? At the micro level, how can individuals get themselves out of situations where their knowledge, skills, and imaginations are not adequately employed? We may need to quit a secure job where we are under-employed and find one that uses our talents, despite the strong messages we will undoubtedly receive (both from others and from our own fearfulness) that this is folly. Retaining a job, even a less than ideal one, is generally regarded as more prudent than letting it go in order to look for something more fitting.

A spirituality for the workplace must have something to say about how we can find our rightful place in the world. We are searching for a place where we can engage our skills and experience, our knowledge, imagination, and passion. And we are searching for a place that neither consumes us with over-work nor leaves us bored and discouraged with under-work. We may need to renegotiate our work situation many times, both the externals of *what* we do and the internals of *how* we do it. We will need many inner conversations with ourselves (and such conversations are the heart of spirituality) about whether we are in the right place at any given point in our lives. And the answers will relate not to external success or any assumptions about what we *should do*, but to a personal sense that there is a *rightness of fit* between what we can offer the world and what work we are engaged in.

Questions

Is there a "rightness of fit" between you and the work you do?

Are burnout or rust-out concerns for you?

The impersonal work world

In our quest for work that fits with our gifts and life situation, the work environment itself may be problematic. Scott Adams's cartoon strip *Dilbert* exemplifies the cynical, conflict-ridden, fragmented world of work that many of us know. There is an incompetent but powerful boss who is not respected by his employees although they outwardly kow-tow to him. There is the nerdy computer geek, incapable of seeing beyond his techie horizons and socially very inept. And there is Dilbert, the alienated worker who does as little as he can get away with, ridicules the boss behind his back, and suffers the indignities of office power-plays and control issues. Through humour Adams caricatures a work world that is crippled by bureaucracy, stifled by rigid systems of management, and undermined by an absence of trust.

The success of the *Dilbert* cartoon suggests that many of us recognize this fictitious workplace. It is particularly within large organizations that the dysfunctional characteristics emerge, as hierarchies and regulations are developed to ensure that the jobs get done and employees are treated uniformly. A degree of impersonality enters, which inevitably separates bosses from workers and tends to create and perpetuate an Us and Them mentality. With a high degree of specialization in work now, people are often also working in isolation from their peers. Metaphorically we have moved from the family farm to the typing pool to the office cubicle, and the impersonal modes of communication made possible by email and other electronic media have further eroded human interaction at work.

In one telling cartoon strip, Dilbert's boss has his employees wearing electronic collars, so that he can track their whereabouts in the building at any time. "Once you got used to working in cubicles, like gerbils," he says, "we knew anything was possible" [Adams 1996, 76]. A common complaint at work is that people feel like rats running faster and faster on wheels, or trapped in the constant performance of repetitive tasks. They may feel obliged to skip lunch breaks in order to get the work done, and a sense of hostility builds up, aimed at those who are requiring this level of output. Managers are in turn under pressure from executives, who are trying to steer their organizations through turbulent economic times with maximum efficiency and profit, and the cycle of resentment and tension continues.

Conflict and criticism

Where community and trust do not flourish in an organization, adversarial positions will often be taken between individuals and between groups almost instinctively. Like our parliamentary system with its government and opposition seats set squarely opposite one another, dysfunctional workplace dynamics deal in conflict and power struggles. And the fallout is cynicism, fatigue, and stress. No organization is immune from the problem of destructive conflict, whether it is a multinational corporation or a convent, unless it consciously works to promote good personal relationships among its members, marked by trust and mutual respect. This is especially true in the touchy areas of expectations, evaluations, and feedback.

Franco's Story

Franco is passionate about his work. He takes his job very seriously, working long hours to accomplish the many tasks he takes on. When asked to accept a new project, Franco rarely says No. Several years ago, Franco's organization was engaged in a strategic planning exercise that was looking at priorities for the short- and long-term. One of the initial activities of the strategic planning process was a survey of the employees to determine the key values of the organization. Franco was asked to lead a task force to conduct the survey and, of course, he said Yes.

The task was complex, with input required from across the organization. Franco's task force conducted the survey and various forums to hear from everyone. They then studied the results and wrote a report. The report was circulated and generated a lot of interest. Franco was pleased to have the work done and felt a great sense of accomplishment. Then things changed. There was widespread criticism of the report. The results were ridiculed. People argued that the survey was not conducted properly and, therefore, the results were wrong. In fact, all that Franco did was to tell members of the organization what they themselves had answered on the survey.

What they were really challenging were the answers of their peers. The people complaining were generally the older employees of the organization who did not listen to the viewpoints of the newer members who now made up the majority. Since they did not listen to the younger employees, the older employees did not recognize these values when they were reported by Franco. Unfortunately, Franco got caught in the middle of this. His report was, in fact, accurate. But Franco took the criticism very personally. He was quite devastated that his work, so carefully done with much consultation, could be viewed as flawed. The conflict wounded him personally and deeply, and the hurt remained for many months.

--- --- ---

What can we learn from this story? Clearly, Franco needed to understand that he was not being attacked — the report was. And furthermore, it was changes in the attitudes of employees in the organization that the critics were really challenging. The strategic planning process had worked — it had found the real values of the majority of employees within the organization, although this in turn had aroused the ire of the minority and caused the conflict that Franco had experienced so personally.

As time passed many of the critics realized that Franco's results were not only correct but insightful and useful to the organization. But they did not give Franco this feedback, or apologize for their earlier blistering attacks. The culture of this workplace permitted destructive criticism without the social norms of respect and courtesy. The criticism of Franco's work was personal, and Franco received it personally.

His experience is by no means unique. In many workplaces conflict takes a heavy toll and goes beyond the level of disagreement or negative feedback. It is as though, while we are at work, we allow ourselves to dehumanize others and to become dehumanized ourselves. So a report is ridiculed, a boss is maligned, an employee is humiliated, and workplace relationships become battlefields where even the minimal respect that we accord our neighbours and friends is absent.

Paradoxically, while wanting to put our heart into our work we must also learn to step back from it, not take it too personally. Franco learned from his experience that he has to think of his work as separate from himself. In the words of the Tao Te Ching, "Do your work, then step back. The only path to serenity" [translation by Stephen Mitchell 1988, 9 — please see chapter 8 of this book for more on Taoist wisdom for the workplace].

The results of work — a report, a chair, a hockey stick, this book, milk, tax returns — are services, products, objects. The results of work are not the people of the organization. We may take pride in good work and try to fix bad work, but we are not the work. We need to be able to disagree without mudslinging, and detach ourselves from any mud that comes our way. Jesus, Gandhi, and other visionaries did not let the conflict created by their work diminish them, and neither did they respond in kind.

I am not my job. I am not the tasks I do at work.

How am I doing?

As we pour ourselves out in the work we do, the feedback we receive assumes huge significance. We have various expectations about how we will be remunerated, promoted, or otherwise rewarded, and our society sends out strong messages about what it is to succeed. The ladder of career success is set out before us, but the reality often feels more like the children's game of Snakes and Ladders as we encounter setbacks, conflict, disappointments, unfair appraisals, dead ends. Because we tend to define ourselves by the work we do, when that work leads not to a ladder going up but to a snake going down, our self-esteem receives a body blow. An expected promotion fails to materialize, and I feel crushed and devalued. An evaluation contains negative comments about one aspect of my work, and that is all I take in. My sense of worth has a skin as thin as a balloon's and is as easily burst.

We all need affirmation and encouragement. We need a sense of how we're doing, what we're accomplishing, how our lives are making a difference. But when we look to external indicators only, such as the status we attain in an organization, or the money we make, or the opinion of the boss, or even the success of our enterprise, we are setting ourselves up for failure because externals are always fickle. Like setting up a ladder against a rickety wall, we wobble and fall when the wall does not hold.

We need to find ways to base our self-esteem on surer foundations, so that no matter what happens around us in the workplace, we are anchored in the knowledge that ultimately our worth is not measured in status, salary, or success, but in our humanity.

Sam the workaholic may need to spend more time looking into his children's eyes and seeing the gift of parenthood, if he is to break out of his work addiction and the associated problems. He may need to challenge actively the expectations that he will work around the clock and sacrifice his personal life. He will almost certainly have to give up the fear that if he does things differently and takes more time away from work, his career will come crashing down around him. Franco discovered that a healthy separation of his identity from his work was vital to riding out a time of conflict.

～～～

Questions

What are your criteria for success? Applause from others? Inner satisfaction?

On what does your self-esteem depend?

A spirituality of the whole person

Spirituality has been defined as that which stops us from getting unglued. It has the power to keep us in one piece, with our feet on the ground. In a complex, fast-paced world where work consumes so much of our energy, shapes so much of our life and gives definition to our very identity, we need a strong glue to keep us connected to what really matters and to prevent us from flying apart in fragments as we race from one task to the next. We work in order to provide for our needs, but a spiritual perspective reminds us that those needs are not merely material. "Seek God's kingdom first," Jesus taught, "and all the rest will be given to you" [Matthew 6:33]. In other words, don't lose sight of the deepest priorities in the midst of the demands of daily life; indeed, fix your sights on those priorities, and the others will fall into place.

Taking a long, searching look at one's priorities is the first step. How are we spending our time? What choices are we making? What is being sacrificed? Is there balance in our lives, with attention being paid to the body as well as the mind, our leisure time as well as our career, our family and friends as well as our colleagues, volunteer work as well as paid employment? It is easy to be carried along on the tide of a culture that puts status, success, and the endless acquisition of material possessions at the centre, and urges us to focus on these things. What brings the other parts of our lives into focus?

A spirituality for the workplace must be one that supports and promotes a holistic perspective on ourselves and our lives. If it serves only to make us work harder and faster, then it is simply another tool in our post-modern serfdom. Instead, it must set us free: free to choose how we work; free to say No when we have to; free to do our work and then step back. In a world of work with so many woes, this is the only path to serenity [Mitchell 1998].

--- CHAPTER 3 ---

A Culture of More

We work not only as individuals in specific workplaces, but also in the context of a wider culture. What does that culture tell us about work, and what messages does it give us about why or how we should do it? How does the culture shape our attitudes toward work, and the environments in which we work? We saw in chapter 1 that the movement from a primarily agrarian society to an industrial one brought massive changes to the way that people lived and worked. In turn, the movement to today's post-industrial, post-modern, hi-tech society has reshaped work in ways we could never have imagined even fifty years ago.

This chapter will look at some of the difficulties and challenges that arise in the workplace now, as a result of a culture that prizes wealth, competitiveness, and individualism, and rests on electronic communication and technology. While some of the issues are as old as human history, such as the desire for riches and power, others are new to our generation and pose problems that have not been encountered before. For example, is our hi-tech world a blessing or a curse? Does it free us to accomplish more and better things or does it trap us in some way? And is our status as one of the richest nations in the world something to be proud of or does it pose dangers to us? As we strive to be successful at work, do we become better human beings or do we harm others in our way?

There are no simple answers to these questions, and it is difficult even to step back far enough to look objectively at our own culture and examine it critically. But one of the gifts of a spiritual perspective is its ability to look at life through another lens, and to hold up our work and living to a benchmark that transcends culture and history. Religious teachings are always somewhat counter-cultural, if they are founded not on the accepted norms of the day but on a deeper truth. So here we will consider the culture in which we work, and begin to look at how a spirituality of work might address and challenge it.

Consumerism

Within a capitalistic nation such as Canada, consuming products and services drives the economy. When we have an economic downturn, people are urged to buy more. After the attacks on America in 2001, US citizens were told that one practical patriotic response would be to go out and spend money. Our federal and provincial governments are constantly looking at ways to "stimulate" the economy into higher levels of production.

We are all consumers. The days of self-sufficiency are long gone. It is virtually impossible to live independently of what others grow, make, sell, or provide. Even the old-order Mennonite communities in Ontario, for example, which refuse to own and use motorized vehicles or electrically powered items, nevertheless depend on the hospitals, shops, and other services in the culture around them. Goods and services are at the core of our culture. As work and life have increasingly become compartmentalized and specialized, so we need what others produce. We have to buy.

But the shift has gone further than that. We are no longer a culture that simply buys and sells goods and services: we are *consumers*. The word implies an insatiable appetite. Getting and having material things has surpassed what we need. Consuming has become a way of life. We actually try to fix problems by buying something. Going to a hardware store and buying a new fishing rod might be prescribed by a wife for a husband who is depressed as winter drags on. "Retail therapy" may be a somewhat comical reference to going shopping in order to feel better, but it is widely practised. Advertisers assure us, "You're worth it," as they tell us to buy this or that product. We are besieged by advertising in newspapers, on the radio, on TV, on billboards, buses, through our computers at work, even in washrooms. Buy! Buy! Buy! The concept of built-in obsolescence has entered our culture, as hi-tech products become outdated at an incredible rate, and we are urged to buy the newest models even if the older ones still function.

Despite efforts by conservationists to reduce waste, we live in a throwaway society. One of the most striking images that captures this degree of waste, and at the same time highlights the appalling gulf between rich and poor nations, appeared in *The Economist* magazine recently. It was a photograph of a garbage pile in an impoverished Asian country. The pile consisted entirely of old computers and computer parts. Small children were painstakingly salvaging parts for recycling to earn an income. Their community had no clean water or electricity, and these children would never have seen or used a working computer, but they were picking over the remains of the world's outdated and discarded electronic garbage, to make a meager living.

A culture of consumerism can trap us. It pressures us to make as much money as we can in order to buy all the things we are told we need. Many university graduates are extremely focused on finding jobs with high salaries. This is due in part to the need to pay off student loans but also to the desire to have a large disposable income. Salary level is often seen as the most important aspect of a job by young people. Consumerism in our culture is virtually a way of life for our youth. Basketball shoes, designer clothes, video games, and other highly advertised merchandise are portrayed as the necessities of life, not luxury items. Shopping is often listed by young people as their hobby, where once they would have listed sports. And the shopping malls of our communities have become the places where youth gather and spend their leisure time as well as their money. And so the culture teaches youth a lesson in materialism that underpins much of the way our society operates.

Young women and men did not create the current emphasis on consumerism. We did. Our organizations, advertising agencies, and media promote celebrities who are paid to wear the designer clothes, drive the fast cars, acquire the big houses. Directly and indirectly we participate in a culture of consumerism. We take it for granted and assume that it is necessary for the economic well-being of our nation.

But consumerism has the power to enslave us and override other aspects of our being. Our possessions so easily end up possessing us. All religious traditions teach that humans are not merely material beings, but are also spiritual. Having things cannot feed the soul's hunger. When a culture's focus is primarily on material things, it loses the ability and willingness to go deeper and consider what is at our core. Buying a new suit may help us feel better about how we look, but it cannot help us understand who we are. A promotion and larger salary cannot fill the ache that comes from loneliness. At best, our consumerism numbs us or distracts us. At worst, it traps us in an endless cycle of wanting and needing more and more.

What does this mean in the workplace? Work is often reduced to the means by which to earn money, not a way to follow a vocation or be of service to the world. We need money in order to live, of course, but when we are spending more and more, and working harder and longer to make enough money to keep spending, something has gone wrong. The merry-go-round is spinning out of control. Consider what happens at Christmas time, for example. Many Canadian families go significantly into debt after buying expensive Christmas presents that they cannot afford. At the celebration of the birth of Jesus, who urged the rich to give up their wealth and find the kingdom of heaven through simplicity and trust in God's goodness, many people overload their credit cards to fill their homes with symbols of affluence. The irony could hardly be deeper.

In reaction to the habit of endless consumption, there is a movement now to promote a "Buy Nothing Day" in the run-up to Christmas and its orgy of spending. For one day a year, people are challenged to see if they can resist the urge to spend – and to notice at the same time how addicted we are to spending. We shop to cheer ourselves up. We buy a candy bar for consolation. We buy a coffee as an excuse to take a much needed break. Like fasting from food, a fast from the habit of spending money teaches us about ourselves and our appetites. And it helps us to detach just a little from a culture that promotes endless acquisition of more.

Questions

Could you go for a whole day without buying any-thing? Could you last one week? What would you miss most?

Are you in your current job because of what it pays you or because of what it enables you to give?

Competition

Just as our society depends on consumerism, so in large part it is also based on competition. Children playing games quickly realize that winning is important. The phenomenon of irate parents at sports matches, encouraging their children to play more aggressively or hurling abuse at the referees, may publicly be frowned on but is re-enacted in boardrooms and factory floors daily. We build competition into our education system: ranking and grading are used to determine which students get accepted into the best universities, which ones receive scholarships and awards. And we send conflicting messages to students: teachers tell students that they can work together on a project, but they must all turn in individual work so that they can be given individual marks.

Building competition into our education system to the degree that we have creates a competitive mindset in every aspect of life. Competition is viewed as natural and healthy, weeding out the weak and less fit. And naturally graduates bring this to the workplace. University and college graduates who are used to competing with one another and striving for first place are less likely to be able to fit into a workplace where collaboration and cooperation are necessary.

Yet advanced level work of the type that university graduates do is now typically done in a team of twenty, thirty, or more employees. They must work for the betterment of the team, not their own success. And they have not generally been well schooled in this. In the workplace, many tasks must be done through cooperation. People who cannot move from competition to cooperation are going to find work alienating.

This is especially true of managers — they must be able to work cooperatively with other managers and with the employees who report to them. A workplace cannot evolve when managers are constantly trying to compete and gain power over others, and have not learned to trust and be interdependent.

The entertainment industry contributes to the problem by consistently celebrating the supremacy of the fittest in a way that would make Darwin blush. Reality TV shows such as the hugely popular *Survivor* or *Big Brother* are all about people making it to the top and to fame and fortune by whatever means they can. Strength and deception are applauded if they bring success. Trust and cooperation are rarely affirmed, and sometimes portrayed as weaknesses.

The business world is typically seen as the most competitive workplace environment. We are all familiar with stereotypes of ruthless and corrupt CEOs, offices like shark-infested waters, and employees working round the clock to win contracts and climb the ladder. But other workplaces suffer from the same basic dynamics when competition overrides cooperation and colleagues distrust each other. Many of today's workers are in contract positions, and feel they have to watch their backs all the time.

Cost cutting is a constant issue, and people know they are expendable. To be "competitive" companies have to get more from their employees with less. The *Dilbert* cartoon strip once again conveys reality with exaggerated humour:

"I can assure you," says the boss to his employees, "that the value of the average employee will continue to increase." Dilbert asks, "Is that because there will be fewer of us, doing more work? I'm right, aren't I?" "Except for the 'us' part," replies the boss [Adams 1996, 80].

Because the culture is around us all the time, like water to fish, it is difficult to see this culture for what it is, and even more so to remove ourselves from it or go against the tide. We tend to assume that it is just the way things are, and we adapt or resign ourselves to what seems unalterable. Sometimes, however, an intolerable situation can be the catalyst for making a life-changing decision and going in a countercultural direction.

Natasha's story

After excelling in school and graduating from university with honours, Natasha found a job in the corporate world. The pace of work was very demanding, and the atmosphere was electric with stress, competitiveness, and a rapid turnover of projects. At first Natasha thrived. The work culture suited her high energy level, assertiveness, and love of accomplishing challenging work. She usually worked alone, and saw no need to develop friendships within the company. Besides, she was too busy.

Natasha had taken out a significant mortgage on her first home when she had started this job. The house was more than seventy kilometres away from the city where the company offices were, and the commute sometimes took her almost two hours. After just a few years, the emotional and physical fatigue began to take its toll on her. She was losing weight, experiencing digestive problems, and suffering from frequent migraines. Her doctor told her the problems were stress related.

A phone call to her sister proved to be the turning point. Her sister asked her bluntly, "Do you enjoy your work?" It was a question Natasha had avoided asking herself. "Well, do you?" her sister persisted. After a long pause, Natasha said quietly, "No, I don't. But I can't quit. I have a mortgage to pay, and I'm positioning myself for a promotion this year. I've put so much of myself into this job, I can't walk away now!" "But what's the point of the house and the promotion," replied her sister, "when you're sick and tired all the time? You're a free agent. Make some choices that will bring you joy!"

Later that month Natasha handed in her resignation to a boss she barely knew, and cleared her desk among colleagues whom she had only ever seen as rivals. No one asked why she was leaving. Today, a year later, she works locally in a small business with colleagues who are becoming friends. She owns a smaller house and has had to make some financial sacrifices. But her health is good and she has no regrets. The environment that had initially seemed so exciting and stimulating had swiftly become toxic, and Natasha *was glad to walk away. "It was dog-eat-dog," she told her sister later. "And I decided to change the menu."*

—~—~—

Questions

How do you view the people you work with? Are they rivals, just colleagues, or friends?

Does your work require you to be competitive?

How does that affect you?

How might you develop more cooperation at work?

Virtual work realities

Another defining characteristic of the workplace culture today, unimaginable a few decades ago, is the world of electronic communication. The ability to communicate globally and almost instantaneously has revolutionized how we work, as well as how we see the world and relate to one another. The Internet has created an invisible web of links among individuals, organizations, and nations. We can sit at our TV or computer screens and see images of events happening on the other side of the world at that moment. We can read messages from people in the next office or thousands of miles away, seconds or less after they have sent them. Internet cafés exist in remote villages. Laptop computers have been taken to every corner of the globe. The reach of our communication is farther and faster than ever before.

Clearly there are many benefits to this communications revolution. A global network of news, for instance, means that international awareness of events and crises is greatly increased. The Rwandan genocide was seen far beyond Africa, even if reaction was slow. The image of the falling of the twin towers in New York on 11 September 2001 was flashed around the world as it happened. People can respond to needs over great distances with enormous speed. Small grassroots groups can be connected with each other without the expense of travel, and can support each other in projects around the world.

At the same time, paradoxically, we are more disconnected from each other. More and more people work at home on their computers, entering data, writing reports, taking conference calls by phone, faxing papers, making and implementing decisions. They may go for weeks or months without physically seeing their colleagues or bosses. The same is true of personal relationships: through instant messenger systems and internet sites, people "meet," "chat," and make connections without ever having to be in the same place together. It is possible to assume a completely different persona, and claim to be anyone one chooses, when there is no visible frame of reference or actual face-to-face meeting.

A whole generation of young people has grown up with virtual communication as the norm. Talking on the phone for hours has been replaced by chatting over the Internet. Parents worry about dangers that did not exist before: chat-room predators, Internet hate mail, pornographic and violent websites. And the anxious parents may have only the vaguest understanding of the technology their children use so expertly. Some concerns are arising, too, that young people's social skills may suffer when they spend so much time in virtual relationships. Why take the time to get to know the student next-door in a university residence, for instance, when you can sit in your room at your computer and chat with your old friends on the Internet?

In the workplace, too, this technology is a two-edged sword. On the one hand, it facilitates the speed and ease of communication. I can email my boss and get a quick reply without having to make an appointment or wait for her phone line to become free. Through the Internet I can access information from a vast array of sources almost immediately, instead of searching painstakingly through a library of books. But on the other hand, the sheer amount of information and communication can be overwhelming. It has been said that ten years ago, a typical secretary's desk at work contained forty hours' work on it: that is, it would take a full work week to deal with all the work and clear it off. Today the amount of time required to deal with all the emails, faxes, and in-coming work would be one hundred hours.

Many of us have experienced the feeling of dread on returning to the computer after a few days away, knowing there may be several hundred emails waiting, all having to be read even if most are destined to be deleted. Electronic communication has opened a Pandora's box, and we are deluged with junk mail, some of it carrying viruses, as we try to do our work. The time we spend at our computers not only causes physical problems such as carpal tunnel syndrome and neck or shoulder pain, but also decreases the amount of time we have available to interact face to face with colleagues. How often do we resort to emailing a co-worker who is just a few paces away down a corridor, because leaving our workstation would take too long?

Not surprisingly, the sense of community in the workplace is seriously threatened. Managers have to make conscious efforts to create it: it does not just happen by itself, because we are working so fast and so much in isolation, with the computer as the only consistently present co-worker. Like the Luddites in early nineteenth-century England during the industrial revolution, who attacked the new machines that were forcing them into low-paying jobs with dangerous working conditions, many of us have fantasized about hurling our computers out of the window and getting back to simpler ways of working.

Collapse

The mid-August 2003 "blackout" in Ontario and parts of the US, when huge sections of the electrical power grid overloaded and shut down, brought home both the level of our dependence on electricity and the sense of freedom that came when the power went off. In so many ways our work has become electronic. Even people pumping gas or writing books or working in daycare centres need electricity: without power, gas cannot flow, computers shut down, and air conditioning and lights go out. But as night fell on the evening of the blackout, the widespread looting and chaos that was feared did not materialize. Instead, a party atmosphere developed as people went outside on a warm, unusually brilliantly star-lit night. Neighbours who had lived side by side for years began to talk to each other for the first time. Parents played with excited children. Candles flickered on softened faces. People took care of one another. Despite the inevitable traffic jams, flight cancellations, and work disruptions, it was the most gentle, friendly crisis anyone could remember.

Once electricity had returned, homes and businesses in Ontario were asked to cut power by one half while the various generators came on line. It quickly became clear that this was not all bad. The supermarkets turned their lights down, which many shoppers found more restful. Businesses turned their air conditioners off or up a few degrees, and the warmth of the summer was allowed in. Non-essential workers were encouraged not to return to work straight away, and many people enjoyed a long weekend. Some people expressed regret that the power came back after only one day.

In the aftermath of the power system collapse, as pundits were saying that the supply needs to be boosted, or that our demands for energy have to be decreased, one thing was clear: our culture of massive consumption is heavily dependent on electrical power. We may shore up the system or curtail our use of it, but the present situation is not sustainable. Like Enron, the giant company that collapsed on itself because of its greed and corruption, leaving investors and employees penniless, our culture of more is built on flimsy ground. It cannot nurture us spiritually, and in fact often sucks us dry. It allows the weak to suffer and the poor to become poorer. The warning words of the Hebrew prophets against the sins of the rich are as relevant today as they were then:

> Can I forget the treasures of wickedness in the house of
>   the wicked,
> and the scant measure that is accursed?
> Can I tolerate wicked scales and a bag of dishonest
>   weights?
> Your wealthy are full of violence....
> Therefore ... you shall eat, but not be satisfied,
> and there shall be a gnawing hunger within you
> [Micah 6:10–14].

The gnawing hunger in our culture is a spiritual one. We are materially rich, but spiritually impoverished. We have gained speed, complexity, and technology, but lost peace, simplicity and community. As we have competed to get to the top, we have forgotten how to collaborate and sustain the foundations below us. Spirituality in the workplace is not necessarily opposed to technology or business, but, seeing beyond material gain and career advancement, it does offer a perspective on life and work that can heal, make whole, and satisfy the hunger.

PART TWO

Simple Gifts

CHAPTER 4

Weaving Wholeness

Integrity

We have spent some time reviewing the challenges in the workplace, and the toll these can take on human lives in terms of problems such as workaholism and burnout, and in terms of the creation of cultures of competitiveness and materialism. Many of us feel fragmented, depleted, and trapped by these dynamics, and are searching for some way to feel balanced and at peace as we go through our days.

A spiritual perspective does not so much show us a way out, as though each of us really belongs in the cloisters, but points to a way through that can be trodden with a sense of purpose and integrity. Living a life of integrity means knitting together the separate pieces of our selves, our work, our activity, our focus, and creating a strong, unified whole. An integrated life is like a tree with many branches but one trunk. There is a sense of cohesion and coherence, and one set of roots holds the whole tree steady and nourishes it. In this way, who we are most deeply is reflected in how we fill our time, how we set our priorities, how we treat others, even how we spend our money. Congruence is what we are after — the coming together of the various facets of our lives in a way that fits, that forms a whole or an agreement.

And yet, as we have seen, we are often far from unity or agreement within ourselves when the pressures of exterior life pull us in different directions. Instead of resembling a tree with healthy roots and a single trunk, we can feel more like tumbleweeds being blown around by the wind. We spend most of our waking hours in a culture that values competition over cooperation, output over creativity, consumerism over simplicity.

The quest for integrity faces us with ourselves as we really are, and exposes the gap between what we say and what we do. It seeks to forge an ever closer connection between faith and daily life. It gets our attention with the twinge of an uncomfortable conscience or the spasm of an aching back when our exterior life is beginning to fall out of step with our internal compass. Integrity is wholeness, which is at the root of the word salvation. Our integrity will save us — from self-deception, from hypocrisy, from the waste of a human life lived in the service of something unworthy.

When we live with integrity we are essentially one person: the face the work world sees is much the same as the face our loved ones, our faith community, our neighbours see. Our roles may be different in the various contexts, but our self is basically the same. Yet we are well schooled in the art of dividing ourselves into a number of personae or masks, according to where we are and what is expected of us. The spiritual path of integrity invites us to reunite the parts and become one; to live by our professed beliefs — to walk our talk.

Toby's story

Toby, a university professor, has made it his goal to treat everyone with whom he interacts with equal respect and attentiveness. When instructing first-year students, he is patient and genuinely interested in them. When reporting to the president of the university he is honest, direct, and relaxed. He is known in his department for not engaging in political game-playing or maneuvering, and is widely admired for his trustworthiness and sense of authenticity.

Questions about integrity

List three of the values you hold most dear.

Would others be able to identify these as your values?

Are you the same person at work as you are at home?

Identity

The quest for integrity sooner or later brings us face to face with questions of identity. Who is the "I" that underlies the separate parts of myself? And who am I apart from my work, my roles in the world? We are at root human beings, not human doings, but we live in a culture that asks first, "What do you do?" not "Who are you?" And we define ourselves accordingly. For someone who is unemployed identity can become a critical issue. For someone who is chronically sick, the term "invalid" may include the sense that he or she has no validity in the world.

Identity, then, is the bedrock on which lives of authenticity and worth are built. "Know thyself," urged Socrates. "To thine own self be true," wrote Shakespeare. The message is clear: without a strong, anchoring sense of self we will always be tossed about on the waves of others' opinions, expectations, and demands. Unless I am clear-sighted and realistic about who I am, I will give away the task of forming my identity to peers, family members, authority figures, or the dominant culture.

In the Judeo-Christian tradition God calls us by name — that is, we are not compelled to become like someone else, someone better, someone holier, but simply be authentically ourselves. In the story of Samuel, for instance, God called the child by name in the temple with such clarity that Samuel ran into his teacher Eli's room, thinking that the old man had called him. The story goes on to say that it was the child, not his teacher, who was able to receive God's message and convey it, because the uncomplicated nature of the child enabled him to hear it clearly [see I Samuel 3]. Simplicity and straight-forwardness are great gifts in our quest for an identity with integrity.

Another story, told in the Gospel of John, concerns Mary Magdalene, the friend and disciple of Jesus. After his death she is called by her name when she unwittingly encounters the risen Christ in the garden. Consumed by her grief, Mary at first fails to recognize him. But as soon as he speaks her name she sees him for who he is, and is commissioned to be the first apostle of good news to the other disciples [see John 20].

In the culture of the day women were not regarded as reliable witnesses, and the women witnesses of the resurrection were initially disbelieved. But knowledge of who we are and what we are to do can give us a courageous single-mindedness in the face of incomprehension and even opposition.

It can be a lifetime's work to settle into an identity that is positive, realistic, and internally consistent. A healthy spirituality promotes the formation of a healthy identity. What psychologist Carl Jung called the process of individuation is supported by a spirituality that includes fearless self-appraisal, compassionate self-acceptance, and courageous self-improvement. The spiritual journey then goes one significant step further and enables the individual to transcend self and become deeply one with all. Love of self is not an end in itself but leads on to love of neighbour and enemy.

What are the implications for the workplace? As we come to understand who we truly are, our inner anchor takes hold, and we can live with authenticity and courage. Our self-worth does not depend on external factors but on inner evaluation. Our frame of reference becomes not the praise or criticism of others but the inner voice. This voice neither judges harshly nor excuses weakly but simply notices when we live in congruence with ourselves and when we do not.

For many people the ultimate frame of reference is God. God is the one who knows who we really are: "O God, you have searched me out and known me.... You discern my thoughts.... You are acquainted with all my ways" [Psalm 139]. There can be a liberating realism with this perspective: humans are flawed, certainly, and participate in the evil of the world; but we are created for wholeness, even greatness. In the words of two more psalms, "I have been a sinner from my mother's womb" [Psalm 51:6], but God has made us "but little lower than the angels" [Psalm 8:6].

The more we become who we were created to be, whether we call this fulfilling ourselves or pleasing God, the more authentic our lives will be. Then our personal agendas of control or self-aggrandizement diminish, as does our tendency to feel wounded by criticism. In the workplace the result is a kind of detachment; an ability to go about one's business levelly in the knowledge that God is the primary audience and all others are secondary.

Sara's story

Sara has a part-time job as a legal secretary. She also has two pre-school-age children. Intelligent and capable,

she has been urged more than once to consider apply-
ing for a more senior, full-time position with the firm, or
to apply to law school. Sara's father is a lawyer, and
she knows he had hoped that she might follow in his
footsteps. "I want to make him happy," she admits,
"and I'm flattered that the firm sees my potential. But I
love the time I spend with my children. They're my
priority right now, while they're little. I don't expect my
father or the firm to understand, but that's okay. I
know that being a mother is more important to me
than climbing a career ladder. I feel that this is the
primary job God has given me."

───

Questions about identity

Describe yourself without making reference to the work
you do or the positions you hold.

When and where do you feel most authentically your-
self?

If you were to be more true to yourself at work, what
would you do differently?

Vocation

Working to bring integration to the various parts of one's life and coming to an anchoring sense of self lead on in turn to the development of a sense of vocation — the idea that the "I," the real me, is not just at work randomly in the world but is called to a certain kind of activity. We often think of vocation as something external, coming from beyond us; the voice of God giving us our marching orders. And there may be a genuine experience of being summoned or invited onto a particular path that ordinarily would not have been chosen. But it is also true to say that our vocation comes from deep within, as a rightness of fit is felt between what we do and who we are. Finding a vocation can mean finding one's own, most authentic voice, or the thread of one's life, and following it as deeply as it leads.

In his book *Callings: Finding and Following an Authentic Life*, author Gregg Levoy points out that most of our experiences of vocation are not dramatic voices from heaven with accompanying pointing fingers or burning bushes, but are "the daily calls to pay attention to our intuitions, to be authentic, to live by our own codes of honor" [Levoy 1997, 5]. We all know what it is to feel engaged, alive, authentic: the next step is to notice when that occurs and to learn from it, respect it, treat it as holy.

Andrew's story

Andrew was a senior manager. He chaired numerous committees, wrote volumes of reports, organized hundreds of projects, and managed many employees, all with skill and accomplishment. But he also volunteered at a local hospice, and that was when his heart lifted and his energy soared. Presented with an opportunity for early retirement, and at the same time suffering from the physical symptoms of stress and deep fatigue, Andrew wrestled with what was "the right thing to do." He knew that he could climb higher in the corporation, but he felt a deep desire to give more of his time to the hospice work. Most significantly, he realized that he was living for the time he spent at the hospice, and enduring the time he spent at work. When that realization became clear, he decided to retire and focus his energy on the hospice. His health began to improve almost immediately.

Whatever its origin, a sense of vocation gives meaning to our work. It engages our passion: we have a commitment to and a belief in what we do. And this fuels our journey through workplace challenges or with difficult colleagues. Without vocation or passion, work is just a way to pay the bills and has no intrinsic meaning.

In following our vocation we can find true contentment. As we allow the heart to lead, the internal struggles diminish and the restlessness, frustration, or boredom die away. In Andrew's case, physical symptoms of stress and "dis-ease" started to resolve themselves as soon as his decision was made to follow his heart and step away from the more conventional path. This is very different from the loud cultural message that happiness comes from our salary or status.

Anthropologist Joseph Campbell used to summarize this process of following the heart with the exhortation, "Follow your bliss!" But his advice has often been too narrowly or superficially understood. Some have heard it as, "Do what makes you happiest and never mind anything else." Or perhaps, "Follow your heart's desire and you will be blissfully happy." But Gregg Levoy makes the wise observation that following your bliss "is more about following than about bliss" [Levoy 1997, 10]. A call summons us to a journey, which usually involves risk, change, uncertainty. We step out into the unknown, trying to discern the path and stumbling and learning as we go.

In the biblical tradition the wilderness was often the setting for this journey — a dangerous, remote area in which figures from Abraham to Jesus wrestled with their doubts and fears as they struggled to follow the call of God. Following a calling is not easy: Jonah fled from his; Mary, the mother of Jesus, was told that hers would be like a sword piercing her heart. But in our callings we find our selves — our strengths and weaknesses, our longings, and our shadows. And God calls us by name, that is, calls us specifically and individually, not generically. You are called to be the person who only you can be, not the person you admire or feel you ought to be. And your natural gifts are very much a part of that, perhaps even more than your acquired skills and knowledge.

Vocation has two thrusts. First, it calls in a deeply personal way and is often experienced as a movement or yearning coming from within. Following one's calling can bring a sense of peace and congruity — a sense that who we are fits with what we do. But vocation's second thrust is outward: in the words of Christian writer Frederick Buechner, it is "our deep gladness meeting the world's deep hunger." There is nothing self-indulgent about this kind of vocation; it always leads outward in service to the needs of the world. We are called by our unique name, and learn to trust our gifts and God's grace in us; and then we are sent out to do the work that is ours and God's.

Because the word "vocation" has often been associated exclusively with the religious life, lay people in secular fields have sometimes assumed that it does not apply to them, that their work is too mundane or worldly. Is it possible to speak of having a vocation to be a letter carrier, for instance? Can a stay-at-home mother be said to have a vocation? Yes. A vocational approach to work is not so much about *what* we do as *how* we do it. Sometimes even monotonous, unexciting work can become meaningful when we approach it as a vocation, as something worthwhile and loving. "We cannot all do great things," said Mother Teresa, "but we can all do small things with great love."

Josh's story

After a lengthy period of unemployment, Josh found work in a hardware store. It was not what he had had in mind as his chosen field – his dream had been to be a professional baseball player. But he needed the secure income to support his young family. A wise friend told him, "Josh, if you can't do what you love, at least love what you do." This helped Josh to approach his work with dedication and give his customers his best attention, treating them with kindness and trying to make a positive difference in his corner of the world.

Questions about vocation

Does your work play a part, however small, in meeting the world's deep hunger, or does it contribute to that hunger?

Do you remember why you chose to do the work you do?

If you have been in your present work for many years, can you renew your sense of vocation to it by seeing where it meets your deep gladness and natural gifts?

Mindfulness

How can we stay rooted and grounded in our sense of who we are and what our vocation in the world is? Many spiritual traditions teach the practice of mindfulness as a vital tool to prevent us from flying apart in fragments or being distracted and blown off course. Mindfulness means not sleepwalking through life, or jumping onto the nearest speeding vehicle of ambition, but living with inner awareness and working purposefully. It means remembering who we really are, as unique, beloved children of God, and letting that knowledge inform what we do and how we do it. Simple meditative practices can be helpful for this, and chapter 9 of this book contains some examples and guidance.

Mindfulness brings soul to our life and our work, because it weaves meaning and intention through them. Then life is not simply a matter of getting through the days, and work is not just doing a job: each can be infused with awareness and love. Consider the difference between eating a sandwich quickly while working at your desk, and savouring a favourite meal unhurriedly, in the company of someone you love. Do you even notice the taste of the sandwich? But you relish the other meal; you comment on its appearance and flavour; you enjoy it and linger over it. Life lived at high speed, with the juggling of several roles such as worker, parent, spouse, can sever the spiritual from the everyday, and result in a way of living that resembles gulping down the quick sandwich. Much of what we do becomes automatic and unfocused. We lose our awareness of why we are doing what we do: it just has to be done, as fast and efficiently as possible, in an unending checklist of things requiring our time and energy.

The practice of mindfulness makes us pause and remember. It calls us to taste, to see, to notice. It invites us to bring attention and intention to our lives, so that we can find beauty and purpose there. "Before enlightenment, chopping wood and carrying water," says the Zen proverb. And we have so much chopping and carrying to do! Our work lives can feel like drudgery. "After enlightenment, chopping wood and carrying water," the proverb enigmatically concludes. Yes, the work remains to be done, but it can be done with awareness, with mindfulness, with love. You can chop wood and know that you are chopping wood, and why, and for whom. You can work in a restaurant and bring it your best intention. You can teach and know why you are teaching. You can care for your elderly parents and notice their vulnerability, listen patiently to their stories.

As we learn to work with spirit and engage spirituality in the everyday, we discover the holiness and wholeness of daily life. Instead of compartmentalizing it into different fragments like a pie-chart with slices marked Work, Family, Leisure, God, and so on, and racing from one section to the next with anxiety or resentment about how much time we spend in each, we can gradually weave together its strands into a single tapestry of life. Identifying a personal mission statement is one place to start: does my life as a whole have a direction or purpose that applies to all its parts? If not, can I give it one? [See chapter 9, pages 182 to 184, for a description of how to formulate a personal mission statement.]

The themes of integrity, identity, and vocation that we have been exploring in this chapter are foundational to the process of healing our fragmented lives and finding coherence in them. If I know who I am and what my life is for, and I pursue that with mindful awareness in every aspect of my days, the tapestry begins to emerge and take shape.

Beth's story

When Beth turned fifty she went on an Outward Bound course. During a week of physically and emotionally challenging activities, including rock climbing, bivouacking alone overnight, and canoeing through white water, she found herself repeatedly coming up against the question, "What is my life really all about? What is it for?" Her experience made her feel alive and connected to the world in a way that she couldn't remember feeling before. "This is how life should be lived!" she kept saying to herself. "This is what life's all about." As she came to the end of the week, she knew that she wanted to take something of that clarity home with her, and into daily life. So she created a simple summary statement of what she saw now as the purpose of her life: to live boldly and engage passionately.

Back at work, instead of coasting along and following the lead of others, Beth began to take more initiative

— including saying No to some ventures, and offering a different viewpoint to others. She put more energy into the work she really cared about, and took the risk of trying new projects rather than staying on familiar ground. At home she began to plan the trip to Europe that she and her partner had talked about for years but never had the courage to undertake.

"Things might look the same as ever on the outside," she commented several months later, "but on the inside it feels quite different. I'm actually alive again, not just going through the motions and feeling trapped or exhausted all the time. On Outward Bound there were moments when I honestly thought I might not make it: I might fall off the cliff, or drown in the white water, and I knew I wanted to live. So now I am, and I'm trying to live boldly and passionately, not halfheartedly."

The wisdom of bumper stickers tells us, "Life Is Not A Dress Rehearsal." This message can either paralyse us with fear of getting it wrong, falling on our faces and forgetting our script, or it can set us free to take risks, go beyond our natural comfort zone (otherwise known as a rut), and live, as Beth wanted to do, wholeheartedly. In Jesus' words, "I came that they might have life, and have it abundantly" [John 10:10]. Each of us has a unique contribution to make to the world, no matter how ordinary; our own song to sing. We are each God's work of art, and living small and safe does not serve that calling well. As we identify our voice and God's, and let go of the messages around us that define success materially, we can live more meaningfully and passionately.

Mid-life and wholeness

It can take half a lifetime or more to understand what our vocation is, and how to live with integrity. Many of us set off on a chosen path, or a path we felt in some way coerced to choose, only to realize part way along that it is not life-giving but deadening. As Andrew discovered when given the opportunity to take early retirement, our hearts may be somewhere else already. The so-called "mid-life crisis" can be a critical time of reviewing our lives and reconnecting with our passion, our vocation, our authentic voice. It can feel like an inner earthquake, as old assumptions about ourselves and what we will do with our lives fall away. There may be just a nagging feeling that something is not right: the pieces no longer fit the way they used to; work that used to be satisfying is now only draining. Dreams may present us with images of death and disaster, or entrapment in prisons. Colleagues may notice a restlessness in us, or a lack of enthusiasm. We may have sudden and powerful urges to run away, have an affair, begin again somehow. Like a second adolescence, mid-life can be acutely disturbing with its self-doubt, uncertainty, and disorientation as we survey the world and try to find a way that is ours, a path that resonates with our heart's longings.

It is as though, during the first stage of adulthood, when

we are busy establishing ourselves and making a place for ourselves in the world, the thread of our lives becomes tangled and our sense of direction muddied. We can lose track of *why* we do what we do, or for whom. Mid-life may then be a time of untangling and reorienting, in order to pick up the thread again in our life and work. Or a new thread may need to be picked up, an aspect of ourselves that we have ignored or under-utilized so far. A woman who has stayed at home to raise her children may decide to enter the workplace now, for the first time in twenty years. A businessman may pursue his dream of teaching at a vocational college. An assembly line worker may choose to go back to school and complete her high school diploma.

Mid-life, then, for some, means a radical change of occupation; for others it is a re-engaging with the same work with a renewed purpose and energy. In Beth's case, the deepest change she experienced was to feel more in charge of her life, more like its author than its observer. She continued in the same work, but brought a new perspective. For her, the trigger into this mid-life transition was the Outward Bound week, when she was thrust out of the ordinary routine of her world and given a way of seeing things with a new clarity. Other triggers might appear to be less auspicious, such as the death of a parent or friend, a serious conflict at work, a divorce, a loss of employment. But even a negative experience has the power to make us stand still in our tracks and take stock, if we can resist the urge to flee. A crisis can push us where we would not have had the courage to go of our own volition.

Traditionally, the senior years are the wisdom years. With

mandatory retirement likely to disappear, and improved health and longevity a reality for many, there is time well beyond sixty or sixty-five for continued activity and productivity. But what will we produce? What will the accomplishments of later life be? The underground rumblings and turbulence of mid-life are an invitation for us to step back, look again, and engage with the wisdom we have acquired along the way.

The goal of all this is not to jump-start tired lives with novelty or a vocational makeover. The spiritual quest is for wholeness — to which the word "holiness" is related. The Anglo-Saxon word "halig," from which both "whole" and "holy" are derived, meant healthy, complete, sound. We long to be whole — healthy not just physically but emotionally and spiritually. We long to be complete, at home with ourselves, engaged in living from the heart. As we find the simple gifts and fresh perspectives of spirituality in the workplace, we begin the journey toward wholeness.

Questions

If your life is a story, what is its plot so far?

Has the storyline changed since you embarked on it?

Does it need to take a new turn now?

CHAPTER 5

Humanizing
the Workplace

Hallowing work

*"Whatever you do, in word or deed, do all in the name
of the Lord Jesus, giving thanks to God the Father
through him"* [Colossians 3:17].

This could be the mantra of a workplace spirituality, the constant reminder that our work can become purposeful, even in the midst of its demands and excesses, if we dedicate it to God. "To work is to pray," the ancient Christian monastic tradition affirmed. Each day was divided into periods of time spent in worship, in study, and in manual labour. Members of the religious communities would rise before dawn to pray, thus offering the whole day to God, and would then balance their communal time with solitary study, their hard physical work with rest, and their service in the world with time spent in the monastery. And all their activities were understood as different forms of prayer or self-offering to God.

In a fragmented society, where spirituality is relegated to a realm separate from work and daily life, this understanding of all activity as prayer can seem nonsensical, even contradictory. Many prefer to see spirituality as a refuge away from work, a retreat from mundane matters, not part of work. Yet understanding the deep connection between work and spirituality is a vital step toward befriending our work, humanizing it, and ultimately hallowing it, making it holy, making it a kind of prayer.

Celtic spirituality has always understood the connection between prayer and work. In the highlands of Scotland, for example, prayers from daily life have been recorded after being used and taught orally for hundreds of years: there are prayers that were said on kindling a fire or milking a cow; prayers said on going to sleep and on rising in the morning; prayers like this one, on going on a journey:

> *Bless to me, O God,*
>   *the earth beneath my foot,*
> *Bless to me, O God,*
>   *The path whereon I go*
> [Alexander Carmichael, *Carmina Gadelica*, vol. III,
> 180–181].

How might our working lives be different if we paused to pray on starting the car, and again on switching on the computer? How might our working relationships be different if we had a silent prayer to say before meeting a client or receiving an evaluation? How might our attitude to work change if we saw, as the Celtic highlanders did, God in all things, the holy in the most secular? Work might then become not what we have to do until we can stop, but that which gives us life, our livelihood in the fullest sense of the word. Rather than taking us away from spirituality, work could be a doorway to a wider understanding of the spiritual.

If our work is hallowed in these ways, then it becomes possible for us to see ourselves not as cogs in an impersonal machine, but as people of God, people with a desire to be a blessing to the world for God, people who — whatever we do, in word or deed — do all in God's name. And as our view of ourselves and our work changes, so too does our view of our colleagues. For they, too, are children of God, whether my boss or my co-worker, my client, or my critic.

Do what you love, yes. But failing that, love what you do. You may love being outdoors, hiking and camping. As a child you dreamed of becoming a forest ranger or a camp counsellor. But the reality is that you became an office administrator. Now you have a choice: continue in that work because of its security and benefits, or leave it to follow your dream. You stay. But a further choice comes into play now: do your work half-heartedly, even resentfully, wishing you were elsewhere, or embrace it, choose to love it, commit to it, bring passion and creativity to it, find God in it. If God is in all things, then no work is too dull or mundane to be a potential window onto the divine. If a crofter can forge a connection to God while cutting peat, maybe you can hallow your ordinary, unexceptional work by dedicating it to God and giving it your love.

～～～

Questions

How could you bring love to your work?

How could you forge a connection to God in your work?

Seeing with God's eyes

Marc is a businessman. He deals with people every day, and used to see them simply as clients. But one night he had a dream.

~~~

Marc's Dream

I dreamed that I was going about my daily life as usual, but I could see the private joys and hopes and sorrows of everyone I encountered. Driving to work I could see the anger and fear in the man who sped past me, aggressively sounding his horn. His company was downsizing, and he was terrified that he would be made redundant and unable to support his family. Then I saw the desperate loneliness of a colleague who treated those around her with criticism and scorn. And I could see the secret happiness of a client newly in love. I knew that I was seeing with God's eyes, and I felt overflowing compassion for those people.

I have never forgotten that dream, and whenever I think of it, I still see people differently, even though I can't know their inner lives. I'm less judgemental and more ready to understand others. I feel as though my heart has been cracked open a little more widely.

~~~

Marc's dream contains wisdom for a workplace spirituality, because it shifts the perspective with which we see others. Instead of assessing people according to their external behaviour, we seek to respect them as complex human beings engaged, as we are, in the difficult business of life. As Marc realized in his dream, this is the divine perspective that sees the mystery of the other behind the conventional mask.

This can be a potent perspective in the workplace, where masks and roles predominate and humanity can be lost. It is the perspective that sometimes emerges in crisis situations when status and results are suddenly made irrelevant by the raw struggle to survive. After the 11 September destruction of the World Trade Center twin towers in 2001, for example, survivors reported a change in the way people treated one another once they had returned to work: there was more gentleness and caring, less impersonal pursuit of business.

Seeing those we work with through God's eyes means saying at least an internal No to the artificial but often rigid divisions between people at work, in order to treat each as a human being, each as a child of God. To paraphrase St. Paul, "There is neither management nor union, faculty nor administration, business partner nor client, boss nor contract worker, for we are all one in Christ." Whatever the workplace salary and status differentials seem to say, we are nonetheless equals in the eyes of God.

But how difficult this is to believe! The boss has considerable power over us; we in turn are acutely aware of who is below us on the totem pole. The human mind jumps so quickly from "we" to "us and them." So we protect our position, either aggressively or defensively, blaming "them" for our woes and thus ceasing to see them as part of us. This is perhaps one of the most difficult challenges for a spirituality of the workplace — seeing others with God's eyes, seeing "them" as God's beloved, and humanizing those we work with, instead of "otherizing" them.

Questions

How often do you use the language of "us" and "them" at work?

What effect does that have on your ability to see all as God's beloved people?

A spirituality for conflict

When relationships at work break down, conflict is often the result. And conflict takes its toll on us through stress, anxiety, fearfulness, and emotional exhaustion. A few thrive on the adrenaline rush of conflict, but most of us find it draining and unpleasant. How does spirituality address the demands of conflict at work? This is where theory and theology meet the messiness of reality, and any spirituality for the workplace must be robust enough to offer something helpful and relevant. If it fails to do so, it runs the risk of becoming unanchored and ethereal — a kind of pietism that cannot deal with the real world.

In the famous prayer of St. Francis comes the petition, "Grant that I may not seek so much to be understood as to understand." And this is a foundation stone for a spirituality that can address conflict. Stephen Covey, author of *The Seven Habits of Highly Effective People*, calls the habit of seeking first to understand "a powerful habit of effective interdependence" whereby we can learn to convert the stumbling blocks of conflict into stepping stones. "When we really, deeply understand each other," Covey writes, "we open the door to creative solutions and third alternatives" [Covey 1989, 259].

Most of the time, most of us seek first to be understood. We listen to others with our own filter, our own perspective locked into place, and we believe that our way of seeing the world is the correct way. So it goes against the grain to suspend the inner monologue of self-justification and try to see things from another perspective. And the higher the stakes are, the less willing we are to try this suspension. But, like the practice of seeing with God's eyes, the habit of seeking first to understand the other has the capacity to change us and open us to new perspectives beyond the logjam of conflict.

—◆—

Rose's story

Rose is a teacher. Her class of nine-year-olds was being disrupted repeatedly by a boy who was aggressive, restless, and emotionally volatile. Rose asked the parents of the boy to meet her for an interview, after all her attempts to settle the child had failed. She prepared herself to tell them firmly that their son's behaviour could not be tolerated, that it was affecting the other children and slowing down the class. She steeled herself to be direct and insist on an improvement on his behaviour, with the threat of the principal's intervention and a possible suspension as her last resort.

She was not prepared for what followed. Into her room at the appointed hour came not two parents but one, an exhausted looking man with a kind but troubled face. After listening to Rose's description of his son's behaviour in class, the father explained that there were problems at home: his wife was ill with terminal cancer, and their son was frightened and angry. The boy had asked his father not to tell the teacher what was going on at home, because he disliked the idea of being pitied or treated differently. He needed school to be a safe haven away from the sickness and loss at home. But he did not know how to handle his emotional turmoil.

Rose was deeply affected by this new information. Instead of seeing the boy as a troublesome brat, she understood now that he was a hurt and grieving child. Her attitude changed immediately from antipathy to empathy, and she found herself wanting to help him, even glad that he was in her class so that she could become part of his support system. His behaviour continued to be difficult for many more months, but Rose now knew why, and learned to work with him instead of pitting herself against him.

～～～

In the workplace most of our conflict arises from adults dealing with adults, but the principle that Rose learned holds: we must be willing to understand the other and learn empathy by taking the time and having the openness to listen to another story. We may be convinced that our version of events, our beliefs, our priorities are the right ones, but unless we can at least listen and seek to understand the other, we are doomed to be two separate voices shouting more and more loudly at each other. This is the sad story of much of the political and militarized conflict in the world.

"Love your enemies," Jesus taught. And it has been said that in loving our enemies, or at least treating them humanely and with respect, we cease to hold the enmity and our hearts are changed from hatred to something more creative. Change is in fact a characteristic of this path, for if we are trying to understand the other, walk in her shoes, see him through God's eyes, we ourselves will be changed in the process. If, on the other hand, our views remain rock hard and unflinching, we have probably not finished the task of seeking to understand. Life is so difficult that we must at least be kind to one another.

Bringing love to our work, seeing others with God's eyes, and seeking first to understand are all foundation stones in our creation of humane workplaces where spirituality is engaged and relevant. Another basic principle, especially in dealing with conflict, is learning to step back and release the ego from the conflict — learning, in short, how not to take things personally, how to detach and be willing to relinquish control. When Franco received hostile criticism of the report he had produced for his organization, his wife advised him not to take it personally. But how could he not? Franco struggled to put into practice advice that he sensed was good but had trouble implementing.

The breakthrough came when a friend introduced him to the prayer for serenity used by many twelve-step groups:

God, grant me the serenity to accept the things I cannot
change,
courage to change the things I can,
and wisdom to know the difference.

Franco gradually realized that he could not change his peers' opinion of his work, but he could change his attitude to it. He began to practise letting go of the desire for approval, and letting go of the feelings of hurt. He held onto the knowledge that he had worked hard and conscientiously, and written an honest report. And he spent a little less time at the office with its destructive politics, and a little more time with his family and friends who reminded him in various ways that he was a decent, lovable human being.

Much of our work stress comes from wrestling with what we cannot control or change. It is easy to feel victimized, misunderstood, ill-used. Our response is often to get hooked by the negativity and enter into it, returning criticism for criticism and sinking to the lowest common denominator of workplace behaviour. Bitterness and cynicism become normal, and work is soon joyless. An alternative response is to try intentionally to maintain our integrity and equilibrium in the midst of stress and conflict.

<hr/>

Kathy's story

In the process of union and management bargaining over working conditions, Kathy was a union spokesperson. The talks became heated and conflictual, and Kathy was disturbed to see individuals from both union and management sides maligning one another and taking entrenched positions. She often left talks late at night, emotionally exhausted after unpleasant and unproductive bargaining. Her goal, however, was not only to work toward a fair settlement, but to do so without resorting to hostile tactics or losing her sense of balance. So she practised meditation before each bargaining session, even if only for ten minutes, in order to calm and centre herself, and she prayed for those engaged in the process, on both sides of the table, and tried to remember that they were all human beings mired in the difficult work of life. When a reasonable offer was made, she urged the union members to accept it, disagreeing with those who wanted to push for more. While some members felt Kathy was too soft, others admired her calm presence and dignity.

Kathy's way is not an easy one to follow. It can be perceived as weak, especially in a culture that promotes confrontation and aggression. Like striving to love one's enemies, it means that we are going against the grain and living by different values. It is the engaging of spirituality in the workplace, not pragmatism or survival of the fittest or meanest or most aggressive. It is a letting go, a stepping back, in order to find the peaceful space in the centre from which we can act freely and calmly.

Questions

Think of a situation of conflict you have experienced at work. Which things can you change? Which can you let go of?

What helps you maintain your equilibrium?

Sabbath blessings

In our technologically advanced age we have an odd relationship with time. On one hand, we control it to the minute and give it supreme importance in our lives, with time saving devices (usually misnomers), time management skills, and one eye always on the clock, digital or otherwise. On the other hand, we claim never to have enough time, and feel appalled by its scarcity. Of all living beings we alone seem to be the ones who are aware of time, and this is clearly a mixed blessing.

But another uniquely human practice is the keeping of a Sabbath. From ancient history we have set aside special, regular time for rest, for not doing. In its religious origin it is seen as a divine gift. "The Sabbath was made for the people" [Mark 2:27]. In principle it gives us permission to stop, to cease our labours not just once but regularly, to take time to find refreshment and renewal. In a work-addicted culture observing a Sabbath in any meaningful way requires considerable courage and trust. We need courage to step off the treadmill, be it the factory floor or the corporate ladder. We need courage to leave our cell phones switched off while we take a vacation. We need courage to say No to more work, new projects, longer hours, despite the allure of more money or higher status. And we need considerable trust that without us the world will still turn, the workplace will still function, and there will be a place for us when we step back into it. Perhaps it is not surprising that the Sabbath is rarely kept in our day.

Yet it is possible to have a Sabbath attitude to work, even when its formal and communal observation is absent. We can be intentional about taking time off and loosening the compulsive hold of work. After all, to turn around the saying of Jesus about the Sabbath, work was made for the people, not the people for work. We can make choices about how and how much we work, setting limits and learning to say a holy No to more work out of gentle respect for ourselves, our loved ones, and our world.

We can incorporate the gifts of the Sabbath into our work days by taking time to eat — and just to eat, not to multi-task; time to read or reflect; time to communicate well with our co-workers; perhaps even time to engage in the creative art of play. So much of what we do is purpose- or product-driven. Can we still remember how to do something for no other reason than for the joy of it?

-- -- --

Alison's story

Alison has developed what she calls "Sabbath reminders" in her work, after years of feeling overwhelmed by the unremitting pace and demands of work, and having to take time off as stress leave. She now keeps track of her hours and makes sure that she has two days a week completely free of work or work-related activities. She takes the lunch break that she is entitled to, and uses it to eat nutritiously and mindfully, and to walk. When her phone rings, she uses a meditation technique she has learned: instead of reaching for it immediately

she breathes deeply and lets it ring three times, then
answers it calmly and without holding tension in her
body. In her workspace she has symbols of peacefulness
to remind her of her soul's need for tranquility and rest,
and she pauses in the midst of stressful work to look at
these symbols and centre herself once again. When she
is at home, she is "unplugged" – away from her email,
fax machine, computer, and telephone.

Alison says she takes herself less seriously now, and
her work more lightly, and has been surprised to find
that she works more efficiently and without the exhaus-
tion and resentment she used to feel.

The Sabbath brings the spaciousness of time back into our view. It is a ceasefire in the battle to fit more and more into the time we have. It reminds us that life is a gift, not a race; a journey, not an endurance test. It enables us to step back from our busyness and gaze at a farther horizon. And this in turn puts our work into a different perspective. Most of us have experienced this perspective shift while on vacation, when the importance and immediacy of our work slips away like an outgoing tide. By incorporating a Sabbath attitude in daily life we can integrate something of this perspective in our work world, and know something of the accompanying feeling of lightness, the relaxing of the shoulders and unfurrowing of the brow.

We live finite lives, and the awareness of our finitude can lead us to try to cram it all in now, do it all today, have it all before the age of fifty. Deadlines cause us enormous stress.

But all this is about our accomplishments, not our being. A Sabbath attitude to our creaturely finiteness teaches us to be, not always to be doing. It treasures each moment and remembers to smell the astonishing roses as we come upon them. It says, like the bumper sticker, "Life is not a dress rehearsal." It brings us back every seventh day, or every seventh year, or every time we refocus, to a sense of the precious impermanence of life where there is no rewind button, only a series of present moments.

Questions

How could you insert Sabbath principles into your life?

If you were to take a sabbatical from work, how would you spend it?

Where do you need to say a holy No in your work world?

Balance

The art of balance is the central skill we require as we steer our way through the world of work: balancing work and family, colleagues and clients, our own needs and the needs of others; balancing mind, body and spirit, being and doing. By seeking balance we are seeking to attune our habits and deeds with our words and intentions. Most of us, after all, would claim to be in favour of humane work environments, reasonable workloads, sufficient leisure time, quality family time: it's just that we don't seem as capable of living it out. We don't walk the talk, and we find that our work habits are out of step with our intentions.

Balance requires a fulcrum, a stable central place of rest. We must learn to locate this inner spot where we are grounded, this perspective that we know is truest, and return to it as often as necessary. We need visible reminders of it in our workspace, like Alison's Sabbath reminders, her symbols of peacefulness. We know this unconsciously, as we place photos of our partners and children on our desks, or pictures of the cottage, a lake, a sunset. We set them out like sacred objects on an altar, reminding us of our deepest loves and highest priorities. But if we lose our sense of connection with them and our understanding of what they symbolize, then they become mere decorations, empty of the power to move us and remind us who we are and what we are about.

A spirituality for the workplace brings us back to our senses over and over again. It affirms the goals that are not related to status, power, or wealth — the things our hearts are restless for, such as peace of mind, creativity, the sense of a vocation heard and followed. It helps us to live more in the present moment, and not to worry about tomorrow. It encourages us to be pioneers of new ways of working, where we walk away from post-modern serfdom to a spacious freedom.

Part of our quest is also for the balance between success and failure, controlling and surrendering, growing and dying. The yin-yang symbol for balance is a union of light and dark, illustrating the knowledge that both are necessary and holy. But our highly developed society has an aversion for darkness and all that it stands for — loss, death, letting go. Much of what makes us unbalanced is the attempt to keep the darkness at bay, and the belief that if we work hard enough, we will avoid forever failure and loss. Fear of these things is a powerful master. Yet for our planet to survive we must learn how not to have, as well as to have; how to give away and give back, as well as to acquire. Endless economic growth may not be viable. Endless striving to climb up the career ladder is not necessarily good for our marriages, our families, our health. So the art of finding balance involves release, and trusting that we will not be annihilated if we let go.

"Do not worry about your life," Jesus told the people of his day, with words strikingly relevant to our own day and its demands. "Do not worry about what you will eat or drink or wear. Is not life more than food and the body more than clothing?" [Matthew 6:25].

It is the "more than" that we are after. It is the "more than" that spirituality addresses. Theologian Matthew Fox, in *The Reinvention of Work,* describes this quest as our inner work, which must balance our outer work in the world. "Once one has a spiritual center from which to work," he writes, "no work is just a job" [Fox 1995, 23]. Our inner work is to connect to what we most deeply value and feel called by, and as we link that to our outer work we hallow it and give it greater meaning and purpose. Sam, for instance, might do his inner work by taking time away from work and listening to his wife and children, as well as listening to his own heart. As he recovers from his fatigue and rediscovers his delight in his family, he might decide to make changes in his outer work by resigning from some committees, seeking a less time-consuming position, or changing his career course altogether.

Balancing our outer work with our inner work, like seeking first to understand another, is a risky business because it transforms us. In some ways it is easier to remain a serf, with our eyes on the immediate future and its material prizes, and our knowledge that we are part of a great company of serfs who receive society's approval for their solid work ethic. But our gravestones are not engraved with our résumés: it is by our loves that we are remembered, not by our hours in the office.

So our inner work, the work of spirituality, is about listening to the still, small inner voice, and being attentive to how we are in the world. When we are burning out, or rusting with boredom, or fantasizing constantly about being or doing something else, or locked in conflict and stress, it is time to do some inner work. [See chapter 9 in this book for some ideas on how to get started with this inner work.]

Ultimately the spiritual path through the workplace leads us to a sense of wholeness, so that who we are with our loved ones is who we are at work, and there is no longer the terrible sense of being in two worlds, with two personae and two pulls. Oneness is always at the heart of the spiritual way. So the great medieval mystic St. John of the Cross could say, "My occupation: love. It's all I do."

Questions

What tends to worry you most and throw you off balance?

How could you bring more balance into your life?

What would it cost you?

CHAPTER 6

Creating a New Culture

Community

Individual survival at work is one thing; transforming the workplace itself is another, and a seemingly much more difficult task. But if our faith has any relevance it will do more than critique the problems of the world and describe a better hereafter: it will reshape the world in the here and now. Spirituality applied to the workplace and engaged on a daily basis is more than a coping mechanism with which to get by; more than a comforting cup of tea for the soul after a hard day in the ruthless work world. It is the means by which we can build the kingdom of heaven in the heart of our day-to-day lives.

We live and work in a culture that is greater than ourselves, a culture with certain messages, dynamics, and assumptions. This culture, in the industrial and post-industrial world, tells us, for instance, what it is to be successful, to be wealthy, to be a leader. It tells us that we should be constantly striving for bigger, better, and more. It encourages us to be consumers with insatiable appetites, no matter what the cost to the environment or to our neighbours in the developing world. It promises us riches, but drives us like a taskmaster and grinds on over us when we fall.

It is easy to see why so many of us feel powerless under this impersonal force. We assume that we can do nothing to change it, only to cope as best we can in the face of it. And yet each of us contributes to this culture. It cannot exist without us. So as we stand back and examine it, and perceive how it helps or harms us, we can make decisions about how we want to participate in it. Jesus' metaphor was that we can be like yeast in a mass of dough: the dough can seem insuperably heavy and immovably huge, but the yeast mixed into it has the power to transform it into something quite different — not a cold lump, but a form of rich nourishment.

This work of transformation is not something we can do alone. To leaven the lump we need to find kindred spirits and form alternative communities within our culture. This concept in terms of faith communities is familiar in our cities and villages: the architecture of religious buildings tends to set them apart as different, and when we go into them, we know we are about to engage in something different from our Monday to Saturday activities. But how do we form a spiritual community in the workplace?

The lunch bunch story

During the economic downturn of the 1990s, an organization employing several hundred workers made scores of them redundant, and found itself in a bitter labour strike as a result. After the eventual settlement, morale was low and the remaining employees were polarized and dispirited. Some of the work stations had been relocated, and a common area for coffee breaks and lunches had been eliminated, so in response a number of women decided to organize themselves into a weekly lunch group and meet intentionally, now that they no longer met casually.

This "lunch bunch" included a diversity of religious backgrounds, but all were looking for a way to feel less like victims of the organization, and more connected to each other. They began their lunch gatherings with a check-in: a chance for each to talk for a minute or two about how her week had been and what was going on in her life. Sometimes they spent the remaining time walking and munching their sandwiches outside; other times they stayed in and discussed a book they had chosen together, or read aloud a thought for the day from a spiritual writer and talked about it. When there were serious concerns about family members, col-leagues, or world situations, they listed them in a prayer notebook, and each one prayed for them in her own time and in her own way.

The group created a strong community at a time when the larger organization had become impersonal and adversarial. It was not a clique with a negative focus and a closed membership, but an oasis, a safe haven, to which others were invited. As the women went through crises with health, family, or work, they supported each other and made their workplace a more nurturing environment. They changed its culture.

———

In the Christian tradition the creation of alternative communities, as outposts of the kingdom of heaven in an indifferent or hostile world, is a familiar concept. As Jesus embarked on his public ministry, he began by calling together a small community of followers. They journeyed together, shared their mission, ate, rested, and prayed together. Even though the group was prone to misunderstanding Jesus, bickering among themselves, and failing to live out the message of God's love, the community was central to Jesus' way of working. He was not a CEO or a lone ranger, but the heart of a group he called his friends. And as that community slowly and painfully learned what it meant to follow his way, through the adulation of the crowd, the shame of betrayal and desertion, and the transformation at Pentecost, the community of the church was born.

As Christians today, we can learn to live out our lives "in the kingdom," embracing as far as we dare the radical principles of caring for one another and ministering to the world, pioneered by the early, vibrant communities of faith. The Christian way winds through every aspect of life, not just the "spiritual" moments or the places and times set aside as sacred. Like the lunch bunch gathering to create a caring and supportive community within the organization, the realm of God seeps through and transforms even the most secular environment. There are as many examples as there are people willing to make the connection:

A local minister goes weekly into a factory in his parish, and, around a core group from his church who are employed there, forms a lunchtime Bible study.

Once a year a retreat is held at a university for faculty and staff, offering a time of reflection and meditation, and providing a space for discussions on finding balance between work and the rest of life, and on nurturing the spirit.

Members of a congregation who work in a variety of settings, from a restaurant to an insurance company, spend two months in Lent visiting each other's workplaces with their priest once a week, an hour before work starts. They describe what they do at work and celebrate the eucharist together at each place in turn. As one member of the group commented, "It literally turned my desk into an altar the day I hosted the group, and I've never seen my work as unholy since then."

Creating community is spiritual work. The kingdom of heaven is among and between us [see Luke 17:20, 21]. As we gather to create intimacy, caring, cooperation, the realm of God breaks through. And our individual sense of vocation can be supported and deepened when we are heard, cared for, held lovingly accountable, and challenged to relate what we do at work, and how we do it, to our faith.

—————

Questions

How could you create a time and place of community in your workplace?

Where does your work most need to be leavened? What feels heaviest?

What might act as leaven?

Creating Inner Community

In addition to the community of those around us, there is another sort of community that affects us just as deeply, and this is the inner community of voices that we carry in our heads and hearts. These are the voices of internal criticism or encouragement, fearfulness or motivation. We walk around with an entire committee of inner voices, many originating from childhood, giving us unsolicited and often unwanted commentary on who we are, what we are accomplishing or failing to accomplish, and what we should do.

We saw in an earlier chapter how fragmented our lives become when pulled apart by the demands around us; but the demands from within us can be equally tyrannical. With an inner audience that is constantly critical, telling us that we are never good enough and will never be a success, or undermining our self-confidence by whispering that we are sure to be found out soon for the failures we really are, our energy for work can quickly become depleted. Similarly, when our frame of reference is an internalized boss, shareholder, or client, we can become anxious and unsure of ourselves; yet when it is a loving God or wise mentor, there can be a calmness and centredness even through difficult times.

An important aspect of a spirituality for the workplace is the creation of an inner community for guidance and support. We may have a clear sense of God with us, calling us and upholding us, but this needs to be undergirded by voices of wisdom who can remind us of what we know when we lose track of it.

Lucy's story

Recently I ran into a period of feeling stagnant and barren at work. There were no major disasters or obvious problems, but I had a nagging fear that my work was accomplishing nothing and that, behind the mask of activity and confidence, I was at best burned out and at worst a failure. I was discouraged by poor attendance at some of my programs on campus, and weighed down by the knowledge that despite the best efforts of my board and myself, we still had a deficit budget.

I began to wonder if I had done all that I could do, and if it was time to resign and move on. But nothing else called to me, and the future looked empty beyond that ministry.

Feeling stuck, I called a meeting of the threesome who form my support group. These are individuals who either work or have worked at the same university as me, and who are people of faith and wisdom. They are not board members or clergy colleagues, and they have no role in the evaluation of my ministry. They are simply there for me to call on when I need to talk through any issues. I can depend on them to be supportive listeners, as well as honest, thoughtful, and probing questioners.

The question that in this case became pivotal for me was, "How are you evaluating your work? Is it by counting heads in programs and dollars in the budget, or might there be other measures?" We began to talk about new lenses to look through: Is my work creative or routinized? Am I working alone or in partnerships? Am I still learning? Am I working with integrity, from the heart?

The questions opened up different ways of reviewing and planning the ministry, and took me off the downward spiral of self-doubt. My mentors, a little wiser and further down the road than myself, objective yet supportive, helped me create a new inner community or frame of reference with which to continue my work. In the weeks that followed, my work gradually became refocused and re-energized.

—————

There is a Jewish saying that over every blade of grass an angel is bending, whispering, "Grow! Grow!" We are being silently and invisibly urged on to bring forth our best fruit, the fruit we were created to produce, no matter how often we forget or stop believing that we have anything good to contribute. "Abide in me," says Jesus in John's gospel. "Those who abide in me and I in them bear much fruit" [John 15:4, 6]. We are not meant to do it all alone, or white-knuckle our way to creativity, but to live and work in community — both the community of those who travel the way with us, and the inner community of those whose voices speak wisdom.

—＜—

Questions

Who are the members of your internal committee of voices?

Which voice tends to dominate?

Which voices of wisdom might you invite onto your committee?

Global community

There is one more dimension of community that we must consider, and this is the global. None of us is an island. What we do at work has consequences for our neighbourhood, our local and national economy, our environment, our trading partners and ultimately our planet. But we live in a culture that tends to have tunnel vision and discounts, minimizes or ignores the damage done to both human and non-human life in the wake of the economic machine that drives our work. The bottom line on a balance sheet is a financial figure, as though costs and benefits relate only to money. But as Matthew Fox points out, "What we regard as wealth today is grossly anthropocentric; nor is it valuable in the long run, for even billionaires will have to live under the same failing ozone layer as the rest of us" [Fox 1995, 10]. So we need to widen our awareness of our work cultures in order to take into account a threefold bottom line that reckons up not only the economic costs and benefits of our work, but also the environmental and global repercussions.

The practice of ethical investing, for instance, has challenged the investment industry to look beyond the issue of maximum returns to the question of the ethics of investing in arms sales, tobacco companies, clear-cutting lumber companies, or Third-World sweatshops. When we engage our spirituality to consider the workplace, we realize that we are part of a larger whole, and what we do at work or with our money has an impact beyond ourselves or our organization's economic livelihood. Jesus denounced the Pharisees of his day for concentrating on the finer points of the law but neglecting justice and love [see Luke 11:42]. Their perspective was too narrow. And in his parable of the sheep and the goats [Matthew 25] he taught that we often fail even to notice the needy around us. We need to widen our circle of compassion.

At the heart of many spiritual traditions is the notion that the faithful can create an alternative spiritual community in the midst of the secular world. We do not have to flee from the world or wait for an escape into heaven somewhere else: our vocation is to create a new heaven and a new earth here, by building up justice and compassion. The faith community is then in the world but not defined by it. It names the social evils around us and lives as far as possible by alternative lights. It seeks to resist the societal dimension of sin (and for us this is often manifested by a greedy culture that exploits, consumes, and pollutes), which is a quagmire at our feet — "the evil powers of this world which corrupt and destroy the creatures of God," as the Anglican baptismal liturgy so eloquently puts it. Where once these "evil powers" were seen as supernatural, now we know they are all too human, and we are implicated in the destruction they cause.

Spirituality that engages with this world and holds a global perspective will have sharp criticism of the rampant individualism of our day, not least because the idea that we are islands of individuality is an illusion. We are in fact interconnected as never before, for better and for worse, through trade agreements, globalization policies, and worldwide communications. Weapons manufactured in Canada can end up being used to kill civilians in Africa. Poppies grown in Afghanistan can contribute to the fatal overdose of an addict in

Vancouver. A shiny new SUV bought one year can add to the air pollution that chokes a child from asthma the next.

We cannot be entirely clean of this societal aspect of sin, but we can make ourselves more and more aware of its dynamics and how we are enmeshed with the "evil powers," in order to disentangle ourselves wherever we can. A spirituality of justice keeps us honest, challenges us to make changes, and offers us a vision of community where no one is exploited or harmed.

~~~

Karim's story

Karim works for an advertising company. Creative, imaginative and persuasive, he has flourished in his first five years there, and enjoys a sizeable salary. Among other clients is the manufacturer of powdered milk for infants. Karim himself has worked on designing advertisements to promote the sale of this milk in an African country. He has been encouraged to choose words and images that suggest to African mothers that the best way to care for their infants is to feed them with this milk, as North American mothers do.

One summer Karim's sister comes to visit, after several years of having worked for an aid agency in Africa. She explains to him that because of this kind of advertising, impoverished African mothers are switching from breastfeeding their infants to giving them bottles; but without adequate supplies of clean drinking water the babies are becoming sick or dehydrated. The powdered milk is often watered down, too, to make it go further, because its cost is high. All of this significantly increases the infant mortality rate.

Karim is dismayed. He had no idea his work was contributing to the deaths of babies in a world of poverty far removed from his. He agonizes about what he should do.

Questions

How far is Karim responsible for this situation, and what could he do now?

Are there any ways in which your work is part of a larger issue of societal sin?

Is there anything you can do as part of the global community to live and work more ethically?

Simplicity

In the morass of ethical questions surrounding our work, we can look for guidelines and seek to understand the complexities of each situation. This is hard but necessary work if we are to be responsible members of the wider community. But perhaps what is needed more fundamentally is an approach based on a radically different standard from that of profit and possession — a way of seeing our lives and our work from a new perspective. When religious communities form, they often embrace a set of defining vows of renunciation, such as poverty, chastity, and obedience. In the workplace and secular world, we might consider taking parallel vows of simplicity, compassion, and gratitude as a way of building a culture or community at work that stands in contrast to our culture of more, me and mine. Formal vows are not necessary, but an intention to hold to certain principles and keep them central can shape our lives and attitudes in profound ways.

A consumerist society says that we must have more and more: indeed, it is our duty as citizens with buying power to spend our money on consumer goods and services to make the economy strong. Our well-being is closely associated with our spending and having. Having also extends to non-monetary possessions, such as *gaining* success, *having* a list of accomplishments, *getting* ahead, *holding* power. There is so much language of possession in our culture, and so much focus on what we have rather than who we are: it is as though we are not human beings or even human doings so much as human havings! What and how much we have seems to be the way that we measure each other and are measured.

But all spiritual traditions warn against dependency on possessions and love of money, because ultimately these are acts of idolatry that draw us away from God, and harden our hearts against those who have not. Paradoxically, the rich in fact become enslaved to their wealth, addicted to having and getting, and unable to see beyond the lure of acquisitions. "You cannot serve both God and wealth," Jesus stated [Matthew 6:24]. He did not say, "You *should* not serve both," or "You *must* not serve both," but simply that it is not possible: "For [you] will either hate the one and love the other, or be devoted to the one and despise the other." And when a rich man who wanted to be a disciple turned away, unable to surrender his wealth, Jesus said to his followers, in words that astonished them, "It is easier for a camel to go through the eye of a needle than for someone who is rich to enter the kingdom of heaven" [Matthew 19:24]. Although riches are often said to be the reward of righteousness, the deeper teaching is that they hinder us in our journey to God.

But renunciation of wealth is a frightening prospect. We imagine ourselves stripped of everything and as nakedly poor as St. Francis or the first disciples, who left everything to follow Jesus. So we often make a pact with the consumerist society we live in: we will continue to be part of it, but we won't have *too* much, we won't feather our own nests *too* richly, we will give *some* of our money away. Before we know it, we are caught up again in the cycle of earning more, spending more, having more — and feeling trapped in the demands of this cycle.

Freedom comes through simplicity, which is close to purity. It means having a single focus, embracing contentment, saying "Enough!", learning how to let go, being grateful, practising compassionate generosity, and finding balance. In the midst of teaching about attitudes toward wealth, Jesus says, in an old English translation, "[Let] thine eye be single" [Matthew 6:22]. Single meant pure, straightforward, simple. If our view on life is single, it is uncluttered, stripped down, focused. Without trying to have it all, we seek a simpler path.

Our culture of plenty has become a culture of both too much and too little — too much to do, too much stress, too much "stuff" and too little time, too little peace of mind, too little rest. "Simplicity," writes Quaker author Richard Foster, "is essential in the way that wheels or brakes or an engine are essential to an automobile.... Simplicity may be difficult, but the alternative is immensely more difficult" [Foster 1981, 184].

~ ~ ~

Thérèse's story

As Thérèse approached her fiftieth birthday, she resolved to make it her personal year of jubilee, after the Hebrew concept of the fiftieth year being a time of release, liberty, rest, and redemption [see Leviticus 25]. She was a working mother with her own business, two teenaged children, and a husband who was a busy professional. "I wanted to review my life and simplify it," she said. "It felt so full, so stretched. I was running in and out of the house, busy with all my activities. I never seemed to have any time to myself, even though everything I was involved with was worthwhile and important."

Her first step was to send notices around that she was going to take a year-long pause from her many volunteer activities. She knew she was beginning to see them as a burden, rather than a giving back to the community. Next she promised herself that she would be at home (without bringing work back from her office) every Friday evening, whether she was home alone for a quiet night, watching a movie with the kids, or spending time with her husband: she would just be there. Over the course of the "year off" she surveyed the houseful of possessions — books on the shelves, clothes in closets, old sewing machines — and asked herself why she was holding onto all of it. She turned her "too many possessions" into money for the Third World by selling books and clothes to second-hand stores.

The possessions that were sold and given away hardly made a dent in all that they had as a family. "We had far more than we needed," she said. "Why had we been holding onto so much? At the end of the year, when I was celebrating my birthday, I thought to myself, 'How did I ever manage before?' The letting go seems easier now; the ability to say No to demands is less apologetic. And for me now the choice to buy anything is more deliberate. I am very aware of the power of advertising and the availability of trinkets to fill the place, plus my own insatiable appetite simply to find some new thing to own."

Practising simplicity can be done as a subversive experiment, a dare, even a game. Can you go one day a week without using your car? your TV? without eating meat? without spending any money? Not out of joyless puritanism, but as symbolic actions or first steps toward bringing a little more balance and justice into the world. For the unemployed, for those on minimum wage or pensions, simplicity is not an option but a requirement, and their relative poverty is greatly increased by the affluence of others all around. Canada may not have the poverty of mass starvation and disease, but the inequalities between social housing and million-dollar mansions, or between run-down inner city schools and private academies, are glaring nonetheless. As we begin to practise simplicity and let go of our desire for more, compassion and gratitude are born.

Without gratitude, simplicity is legalistic and sour, a duty, not a joy, born of obligation or guilt. Gratitude frees us to sit lightly amid our possessions and our accomplishments, because in the act of saying, "Thank you," we acknowledge that we are not self-sufficient or necessarily deserving. All is gift — and the gifts are meant to be shared. Mary Jo Leddy, Christian writer, teacher, and refugee advocate, writes, "Radical gratitude begins when we stop taking life for granted. It arises in the astonishment at the miracle of creation and of our own creation.... It awakens the imagination to another way of being, to another kind of economy, the great economy of grace in which each person is of infinite value and worth.... Gratitude leads us to action" [Leddy 2002, 7, 8].

The action Leddy speaks of is always that of compassion. Gratitude and compassion are like two steps in the same dance: gratitude opens our hearts, makes us magnanimous (literally, "big-hearted"), and enables us to care more deeply and share more generously. When simplicity is the music, the dance becomes fluid and natural because we have less to carry around with us and weigh us down.

Questions

In what way does your life need to be simplified?

What would you have to let go of?

What would you gain?

Freedom

Much of the stress we live with in the workplace and in our culture comes from a sense of being trapped, of having no choice but to work harder, run faster through the day, fit more tasks into less time. At the same time, we believe that this is the responsible thing to do, if we want to be able to provide security and plenty for ourselves and our loved ones. So we stay in jobs we hate, or we exhaust and dispirit ourselves in work that consumes too much of us. From this perspective, liberation looks like escape — early retirement, a big lottery win, a retreat to a cottage somewhere else, or a complete inner detachment where we withdraw our energy from our work and just show up, do it, and go home.

But might there be another sort of liberation? Is it possible to find freedom *within* our work, even as we wrestle with it and pour ourselves into it? Author Gordon MacKenzie, once employed by Hallmark Cards as its self-styled Creative Paradox, uses the graphic image of flying in orbit around a giant hairball: "It is the nature of Corporate Gravity to suck everything into the mass," he writes. "Many ... succumb to the pull of this relentless gravity. They are the ones who, suspended in the gray sameness of the bowels of the institution, wonder, 'What year is it?' (So much for the energy of their careers.) ... Orbiting is ... vigorously exploring and operating beyond the Hairball.... To find Orbit ... is to find a place of balance ... without becoming entombed" [MacKenzie 1998, 31–33].

We do not have to walk away from our jobs, or endure them bravely, to be free. We *do* have to disentangle ourselves from total identification with our work and learn to give of ourselves freely and generously, but without depending on our work to define us or imagining that our work can give us everything worthwhile in life. We need to accept the freedom to make choices — choices about *how* to live, rather than slogging through life without lifting our heads up. We need the courage to respond to our callings and follow where they lead, instead of following a certain fixed script handed to us (or so we imagine) by our circumstances.

"Imagine the freedom!" says the lottery commercial. But we are already free. At this time, in this society, we have unparalleled freedoms. What makes us unfree is fearfulness: the animal fears deeply encoded within us that there might not be enough food, shelter, security; the fears that keep us awake at night and entrapped by day.

Imagine, instead, the freedom of exchanging fear for trust. Imagine making choices about your work and your lifestyle that promote health, creativity, and community. Imagine choosing to have less in order to be more. Imagine, as poet Denise Levertov does, living in the arms of God:

> *To float, upheld,*
> *as salt water*
> *would hold you,*
> *once you dared.*
> *To live in the mercy of God*
> [Levertov 1997, 31–32].

We grow gradually into what we can become. It takes time and practice, as well as trust, to work with spirit and to live with simplicity and gratitude as our guiding lights. Shortcuts are usually illusory, but so is our sense of powerlessness when we feel overwhelmed by our work and its culture. We do have choices. And we can learn courage.

--- CHAPTER 7 ---
The Christian Contribution

Throughout this book we have been referring to the sayings of Jesus because we write from the perspective of Christians in the workplace. This chapter will go more deeply into that perspective, as we look at the teachings present in the gospels and in later Christian writings about how we can engage our faith as we live and work in the world. Christianity has an apocalyptic strand running through it, where the focus is on the end of the world and the judgement that follows; but it has much to say about how to be in this world now. It is in fact fair to say that it is a "this-worldly" religion, as much as – or more than – an "other-worldly" religion. This is certainly the case when the subject is work. In direct teachings, as well as in stories, parables, and by example, a Christian spirituality of work emerges that is rooted in a keen sense of what matters most – of seeking first God's way, and allowing the rest to follow on from there.

Despite the emergence of later regulations in the Christian community (a prohibition of any form of work on the Sabbath in certain communities, for example), the gospels do not lay down rules so much as set forth an attitude to work, a perspective on life that determines priorities, behaviour, and so on. We have touched on some aspects of this perspective in earlier chapters. In the first part of this chapter we will use the Gospel of Luke as the primary source, as we explore how Christian discipleship shapes daily life and work. In the second part we will look at a work ethic that is seen as characteristically Christian (Protestant), and at an emerging theology of work for our time, in which we become co-workers with God.

Repentance: Living the old life a new way
[Luke 3:1–18]

Near the beginning of Luke's account of Jesus' life, John the Baptist bursts onto the scene with his baptism of repentance as he prepares the way for the coming ministry of Jesus. His message is clear: "Repent! Turn around! Get ready!" Among the crowd, some people ask him what they should do: it is as though they, like us, need specific guidelines in their lives, not just an imperative to repent. And John's admonitions are very practical: they should share food and clothing with those who have none; tax collectors must collect no more than is required; soldiers must not abuse others with their power, and must be satisfied with their wages.

Repentance, then, does not necessarily mean abandoning

the old life to embrace something totally different, but living the old life in a new way — with compassion, integrity, and contentment. It is the greed and violence woven through our lives that corrupt; the desire to hoard what we have for ourselves; the easy ways in which those with power oppress those without. In a contemporary setting John the Baptist might have admonished those with secure jobs to support generously the work of programs for the unemployed; or urged those in management positions to remember that their subordinates are people too; or called on company executives to give their employees a fair wage rather than raising their own salaries.

These are not uniquely Christian work ethics, but they set the basic foundations for a Christian way of living when we ask what it means to repent and prepare to follow Christ. Minimally, there must be justice and generosity. How we live this more and more deeply is a lifetime's work.

Callings
[Luke 5:1–11, 27–32]

As Luke's story unfolds, Jesus begins to call disciples to follow him. These are classic tales of vocation, involving a radical redirection or redefinition of life. In the account of the calling of the fishermen, Simon, James, and John, the invitation from Jesus is to go from what they have been doing and take a new direction — to go from catching fish to catching people; from knowing the water and its harvest to understanding the human heart and its yearnings. Periodically these fishermen go back to the waters — for transportation, rest, or a return to what is familiar: at one level they remain fishermen at heart. But they become much more, as they learn from Jesus and allow themselves to be challenged and changed. For Levi the tax collector, the change is absolute, and he walks away from his work for good. For all of them, as well as for the others who became part of the group, following this teacher was the start of a new and vitally engaging life.

For us, the disciples represent those who receive a vocation that cannot be ignored and that turns our world on its head. Nothing can be quite the same again. It requires courage, the willingness to take a risk and step out into the unknown. We may feel like going back to what is familiar, but something impels us forward again. The change in direction may happen once in a lifetime, or several times. It may cost us our friends and our retirement dreams, as we move away and follow a different path. But there can be joy in knowing we are choosing to go down the path, no matter how much fear and trembling accompanies that.

Levi threw a party when his mid-life crisis came. It is a time for celebration when a calling (perhaps long resisted or hidden) is accepted. In our culture we tend to limit the concept of callings to religious vocation, and celebrate with ritual when a person is ordained or enters the religious life. How different it might be if we created rituals to bless, support, and celebrate those embarking on secular careers, making career transitions, or entering retirement! We need the support of community, as we venture out after a calling, and we need a spirituality that connects our work in the world to the whisper deep in our hearts.

Being and doing
[Luke 10:38–42]

Of all the words of Jesus in the four gospels, his words to Martha perhaps resonate most deeply with those of us who feel a longing for peace and holiness: "Martha, Martha, you are worried and distracted by many things; there is need of only one thing." The sisters Martha and Mary were friends and disciples of Jesus, who opened their home to him. In this story Martha is trying to be hospitable during one of Jesus' visits, and is busy with many tasks while Mary sits quietly at Jesus' feet and listens to him. The tension builds inside Martha, until she comes out with a plea for Jesus to tell Mary to help her. His reply instead offers Martha freedom from her self-imposed busyness.

Traditionally this story is retold as a description of the contemplative religious life, represented by Mary, and the active life in the world, personified by Martha. When Jesus goes on to say, "Mary has chosen the better part," the implication is that the cloistered life of prayer and contemplation, withdrawn from the world and its cares, is the higher calling. But it is possible to see both Martha and Mary as parts of ourselves, whatever occupation or calling we have undertaken. Mary, then, is the loving, centred heart, resting in peace and attentive stillness, while Martha is our busy, engaged mind and body, running from one task or thought to the next, often tired and distracted, sometimes resentful. The old tension between the contemplative and the active life is being played out within us all the time.

There are times of activity and times of quiet in all our

lives, and we are by nature more drawn to one than to the other. But the balance is crucial. In our work we become bored or disengaged if we hold back from activity. Or we may become intolerably "other-worldly" if we refuse to get our hands dirty and share in the sheer hard work of living. Alternatively, we burn out and become bitter if we try to undertake everything ourselves, with no self-care or time to rest and be replenished. "There is need of only one thing," said Jesus. He did not define what it was, but Mary had chosen it. To be able to be still and not-do, to listen and learn wisdom, to know when to be busy and when to cease — these are skills or gifts that lead us toward the "one thing." As Luke's gospel continues, it becomes clearer what that one thing is.

The heart's treasure
[Luke 12:13–34]

With a parable and then with direct teaching, Luke portrays Jesus as spelling out the core of the Christian way through life: it is a matter of where our hearts are. The parable tells of a rich man who seems eminently prudent by usual standards: he has land that yields plenty, so he builds large barns to store it all, then relaxes and prepares to enjoy himself with the "Eat, drink, and be merry" recipe for good living. This sounds like an ideal situation and an enviable combination of fruitful work and well-earned leisure.

But the sting comes at the end of the parable, when God says to the man, "You fool! This very night your life is being demanded of you. And the things you have prepared, whose will they be?" The folly of the rich man is to place his trust in material security and turn his face away from the fragility and uncertainty of life. He has been living as though death could be kept at bay by wealth, and life were all about indulging oneself in whatever goods can be acquired. But Jesus introduces the story by saying, "One's life does not consist in the abundance of possessions." Superficially the character in the parable is rich and self-reliant, but spiritually he is impoverished or, as Jesus puts it, "not rich toward God." Materialism and superficiality go hand in hand, and the soul thrives on neither. A life of faith is a life lived deeply, with a focus and heart fixed on God.

Following the parable, Jesus teaches the disciples about trust in words that are as needful today as two thousand years ago. He urges them not to worry about their lives from the point of view of food, clothing, and possessions, but to learn a radical dependence on God based on a knowledge of God's abundant generosity. "Do not be afraid, little flock," he says, "for it is your Father's good pleasure to give you the kingdom." The tight anxiety of each day can give way to a calm assurance that we are blessed, cared for, and loved by One who knows all our needs, and whose very nature is to give without measure. At the same time, we are to be as generous in return: "Sell your possessions, and give alms." So this is not the carefree self-indulgence of the rich man who thinks he has nothing to worry about: it is the freeing of the heart from anxiety so that it can open to others and to God.

Love is at the root of faith — indeed the word "believe" comes from "lief," meaning love. We believe in, or put our faith in, that which we give our hearts to. Where are our hearts fixed? Where do our thoughts habitually drift, or our fantasies lead us? What motivates us? What is most dear to us? We need to recognize the pulls on us, the deep attractions or needs on which we build so much of our lives. The desire to provide materially for oneself and one's family is a very deep-seated one, perhaps especially for men. But does it draw us eventually away from trust in God? Does the pursuit of security become habitual and endless, where there is never quite enough, never the confidence that God can be relied upon? Work can easily become a treadmill then, which we dare not step off for fear of imminent disaster and poverty.

Jesus' teaching about trust is an invitation to let go and dare to believe in — to give our hearts to — something deeper than material concerns; to strive for or seek God's kingdom first, and let the rest be the details that follow.

Working with Faithfulness
[Luke 12:35–48]

The early Christian writers assumed that the end times were coming, when Jesus would return in power and glory to judge the world. An urgent issue was therefore how to keep believers focused on their faith and ready for the day of reckoning. Two millennia later the sense of urgency has largely gone, but the fundamental question remains: How can we live and work with a centredness based on our spirituality, when daily concerns blur the focus so quickly?

In the parables of the watchful and faithful slaves, Luke records Jesus' stories of preparation, attentiveness, and fidelity.

He uses the idiom of slave and master, and while we might choose a different image, the virtues are as relevant today as then. The faithful slaves are those who stay alert and ready to do their work, even in their master's absence, and who carry out their responsibilities with the same self-discipline and care that he would expect of them. In short, they work with faithfulness when there is no one to drive them or oversee them.

These parables are not aimed at producing submissive workers for faceless organizations, but are, as always, teaching us about ourselves. We are the master and the slaves. We may have a great desire to live simply, for instance, but can we actually carry this desire out in day-to-day life and work? In Thérèse's case, her fiftieth birthday jubilee gave her the impetus to review her life, sell some of her possessions, and clear more time for family. The challenge then was to continue in faithfulness to the spirit of her decisions the year after, and the years following. Marc, the man who dreamed that he could see with God's eyes the inner suffering of people around him, had to learn to integrate this vision into his life long after the dream had faded. On the occasions when fatigue and stress wore away at him, he had to summon up the memory of the dream and its impact on him, in order to find compassion once more.

Borrowing language from the parables, it is a question of mastery — training ourselves to hold true to our deepest and best intentions, so that we live more and more in tune with our faith. One popular method of practising this today is by asking, "What would Jesus do?" The WWJD initials appear on buttons, jewellery, cars, wristwatch straps, computer screen savers, as their owners remind themselves repeatedly whose example they follow. They are not slaves with an absentee master, but followers of Christ in an age that whittles away at faithfulness and exerts a magnetic pull toward its secular values. What would Jesus do in a workplace situation of conflict? What would Jesus do when overwhelmed with a heavy workload? What might a Christian do, as a faithful follower of Jesus, when tempted to get ahead by stepping on those in the way? There may not be widespread belief among Christians that Jesus could return at any moment, but the practice of constantly reorienting oneself to align with his teachings can bring a deep faithfulness into the mundane details of life and work.

Work and talents
[Luke 19:11-26]

In another parable about slaves entrusted with duties while their master is away, Luke tells a story that we commonly know as the parable of the talents. Three slaves are given varying amounts of money, and later are judged on how they use it. The two who make more money are rewarded, while the third who merely hides his money and returns the original sum to his master is punished.

The fact that the word "talent" now means gift or natural faculty, rather than an amount of money, indicates the way in which this parable has long been understood. It is about how we use the skills or gifts we have, whether we develop and engage them, or play safe and hide them away for fear of failure. Clearly this has great relevance to the world of work.

In the workplace our talents can be used to the full, stretched and explored, or they can be passed over, under-utilized, redundant. We may choose work on the basis of how much or how little it will use our talents. For example, a person with poor self-esteem may consistently choose work below his capabilities, believing that he cannot deal with more responsibility or come up with creative ideas. Or another might apply for a position well above her present one, confident that she has much to offer and eager to learn more and grow professionally. There are many examples, on both sides of the gender divide.

The parable encourages risk. Two slaves make their money grow by trading or doing business — an activity that can bring riches or poverty. But one chooses not to risk at all because he is so fearful of losing his master's money. This one forfeits even what he began with, when the master takes it away from him and gives it to one of the others. We are not dealing here with rules for playing the stock market, or for becoming successful entrepreneurs: this is about how much we dare spread our wings, engage our God-given talents, and live fruitfully and wholeheartedly.

There is a false security to playing it safe all the way through life, not risking, not daring, not exploring the possibilities before us. We are both cheating the world of our gifts this way, and robbing ourselves of the opportunity to become more like the person we were created to be. A meditation teacher once asked his student, "Why haven't you expanded?" after she had been learning from him for ten years. He was not referring to the small business that she ran, but to the smallness of her view of herself, her purpose in the world, and her heart's capacity to love. In author Marianne Williamson's words, which Nelson Mandela quoted in his inauguration speech, "Your playing small doesn't serve the world."

In a spirituality for the workplace we must ask: Is our work expanding us? Is it increasing our gratitude to God and opening our hearts more deeply in service to the world? Does it give us scope to risk and grow, or is it the hiding place from where we live cautiously? False modesty about our talents is a form of ingratitude or unbelief: we refuse to accept that God has given us gifts, and we do not use them for good. Conversely, priding ourselves on our talents is forgetting that their origin is in God, not in us. When we work instead with humility (derived from the Latin word "humus," the ground) we are down-to-earth about our talents, not bragging or minimizing but able to see what our talents are and willing to develop them, with gratitude to God and love for the world.

An evolving work ethic

Perhaps the best-known contribution from Christianity to the world of work is what has become known as "the Protestant work ethic." The term was coined in 1904 by sociologist Max Weber when he published his classic study of the rise of capitalism and the work ethic that supported it. He theorized that it was the theology of the Protestant Reformation in Europe in the sixteenth century that created this ethic that promoted hard work, denounced idleness, taught acceptance of one's station in life, and distrusted pleasure. The Protestant work ethic produced, according to Weber, "sober, conscientious, and unusually industrious workmen, who clung to their work as to a life purpose willed by God" [Weber 1958 ed., 177].

Prior to the Reformation, work had generally been seen as a curse, following the story in Genesis of Adam's punishment after the sin in the Garden of Eden [Genesis 3]. God had decreed that henceforth Adam should toil by the sweat of his brow in order to live. The pious in Christendom sought to escape this curse by living in monasteries and immersing themselves in a life of prayer, while in the secular world the rich lived in self-indulgent luxury and the poor endured Adam's curse of hard labour. Work was seen as having no intrinsic value, but was an evil that only few could avoid.

The reformers challenged this by stating that work could be an expression of one's duty to show neighbourly love, and that laziness, not toil, was cursed. German reformer Martin Luther believed that different kinds of work were equally valid vocations, as God called each individual to a specific task in life. So even manual labour, formerly despised, could be a fulfilment of God's will. Hard work was not the penalty for sin, but was the expression of gratitude to God for the gift of salvation.

Today this Protestant work ethic is often considered to be an approach to work that is driven, guilt-laden, and joyless. It is viewed as lying at the root of workaholic tendencies, as well as causing miserliness by putting off till an indefinite future any enjoyment of the fruits of hard work. The generations born after the post-war Baby Boom typically reject this work ethic, and pity or deride their forebears for living by it. Weber himself saw that an ethic of self-denying hard work could become a prison; and after the industrial revolution, when workers had long since lost their religious motivation and were employed in impersonal factories at low wages, he described them as "specialists without spirit, sensualists without heart," trapped in the "iron cage" of a capitalist system that cared only for profit and abandoned the poor. Small wonder that the Protestant work ethic is usually seen as a negative contribution of Christianity!

But the movement away from seeing work as a curse was an important one. As the work ethic has evolved, the kind of work we do and the conditions in which we do it have become central concerns, and there is an understanding that work can be meaningful and rewarding, in more than financial ways. Unions, human resources personnel, managers, and others have all played a vital part in making work safer, more fairly paid, and more satisfying. And as women have entered the workforce in increasing numbers since World War II, their contribution to the conversation about work has emphasized the value of creativity as well as profit, working with others as well as developing independence, and progressing steadily rather than working super-human hours to attain fast results.

A work ethic is therefore an evolving part of our societies, and continues to be formed and reformed, beyond the legacy of the biblical writers and the Protestant theologians. As we ask questions about why we work and how we work, the "right" approach is itself a work in progress. In this post-industrial age of the global village, a work ethic must embrace and promote virtues that were not even considered relevant fifty or one hundred years ago — the virtue (or imperative) of environmental sustainability, for example, or of fair international trading practices. Hard work and deferred gratification may have fuelled the Reformation age and beyond, but they are not enough to save our planet and bring justice to all now.

Work as co-creating with God

A theme in Christian writings about work, which has been present throughout its history but is only now coming to prominence, is the idea that human beings are co-creators with God in our work. God works what Matthew Fox calls "the Great Work of the universe," and we are partners in that work. Our role is not to be cursed labourers or driven profiteers or meaningless cogs in a machine; we are engaged with God in the work of bringing creativity, compassion, and justice into the world, in ways from the spectacular to the tiny. No work need be irrelevant to that greater work.

Fox writes: "To say that we are co-creators with the Spirit is to say that a wild and mysterious thing happens when we go about our work. Whether the work be handing out safe sex information, helping the homeless build their own habitats, planting a garden, learning a song, raising a child, teaching adults, or policing the streets, all of it contains more mystery than problem" [Fox 1995, 123]. The mystery Fox is referring to is the knowledge that we are working with the Holy Spirit, with God, if we go about our business as a labour of love. Just as the Celtic Christians developed prayers for every mundane activity in their lives, so we can sanctify our work by recalling that we are co-creating with God, and our work is part of the Great Work of the universe.

Without this perspective, our work can become too small.

Then, in Fox's words, "it contains no mystery, no deep passion ... no wisdom, no real truth. It is drudgery without meaning; it is sweat without purpose; it is duty without play; it is toil alone that bears no fruit ... it is not bigger than we are, calling us to expand.... When our work is too small it lacks Spirit" [Fox 1995, 122].

Working with Spirit means identifying how our work connects to God's work. It does not need to be religious work (as a missionary, minister, or nun, for example), nor does it have to be grand and public. It is about recognizing that as we work, God works with us. In fact, as the medieval mystic Meister Eckhart says, "Just as I can do almost nothing without God, so too God can accomplish nothing apart from me" [Fox 1983, 93]. God's great work of creativity, compassion, and justice is ongoing, and depends upon us to go forward. Can we view our work in this light? And can we allow that to focus our work, or direct our energies, so that we are not wasted in work that is too small?

In his book about work, Matthew Fox includes an epilogue with a "Spirituality of Work Questionnaire." It contains many thoughtful, searching questions about how we approach our work and what our work does to us and to the world. We close this chapter with a question of our own:

Can you say in one sentence how your work is part of God's great work of bringing creativity, compassion, and justice into the world, and can you be mindful of that connection more and more as you work?

---CHAPTER 8---

Wisdom from the World's Religions

This chapter must begin with a qualifier: it is not by any means a comprehensive summary of all the major world religions and what they have to say about work. Rather, it presents a selection of insights we have found in faith traditions other than our own, which expand and deepen our understanding of what it means to work with spirit. Some of these teachings assume a belief in God, others do not; but all contain wisdom that is as relevant today as it was centuries ago when the texts were originally written. We offer it with the humility of knowing that we are glimpsing only a tiny portion of the great contributions of these faiths, and that our understanding of them is doubtless partial and limited.

Jewels for Daily Life: Buddha's Five Precepts

Vietnamese Zen Buddhist monk and writer Thich Nhat Hanh has popularized Buddhist teaching in the West without making it superficial or disconnected from its Eastern roots. In more than thirty books he has set out clearly and simply the heart of the Buddha's wisdom in ways that modern Western readers can grasp and begin to practise. He is committed to interfaith dialogue, believing that it is an essential step on the way to global peace. "We need to live deeply our own tradition and, at the same time, listen deeply to others. Through the practice of deep looking and deep listening, we become free, able to see the beauty and values in our own *and* others' tradition" [Nhat Hanh 1995, 7].

Nhat Hanh has rephrased for contemporary times Buddha's Five Precepts, teachings for daily life akin to the Ten Commandments. In their traditional form, they are:

1. Refrain from taking life.
2. Refrain from taking what is not freely given.
3. Refrain from sexual harm.
4. Refrain from false speech.
5. Refrain from reckless intoxication.

He describes these precepts not as rigid rules but as "jewels that we need to study and practice" [90]. Instead of presenting them as prohibitions, Nhat Hanh sets them out as virtues to be cultivated: compassion and non-violence, loving-kindness and generosity, sexual responsibility and integrity, truthful speech and deep listening, and good health and mindful consuming. Each of these virtues has relevance to the world of work, either directly or indirectly.

The first precept concerns reverence for life, and addresses the fact that killing and destruction are all around us, in subtle forms as well as overt. How can we cease to be part of the violence? First we must see it for what it is and where it is. Does our work contribute in any way to the suffering of the world? Does our way of working harm others or the environment? Do non-human lives suffer because of our work? Buddhism stresses the principle of inter-being, the understanding that all things are interconnected; and so any single action affects the whole. We may not be directly involved in the destruction that brings so much suffering into the world, but we must look deeply to see whether we are indirectly involved or are condoning violence. In fact, as Nhat Hanh points out, none of us can live perfectly non-violent lives. But by cultivating compassion and non-violence, and having the courage to ask searching questions about the effects of our work on the world, we can move toward deeper reverence for life.

The second precept encourages us to work for the well-being of all, especially by not stealing and by practising generosity. The core of this jewel for a spirituality of the workplace concerns our use of time. Thich Nhat Hanh observes, astutely, "People of our time tend to overwork, even when they are not in great need of money. We seem to take refuge in our work in order to avoid confronting our real sorrow and inner turmoil. We express our love and care for others by working hard, but if we do not have time for the people we love, if we cannot make ourselves available to them, how can we say that we love them?" [Nhat Hanh 1995, 94].

He tells the story of a wealthy man who asked his little son what he would like for his birthday. "Daddy, I want you!" was the boy's reply. His father was often away from home, working to provide for his family; but in effect he was stealing from his son the unrepeatable time of father and child. Cultivating generosity is, therefore, not just about material kindness: it is also about giving the gift of our presence.

The third precept, about sexual responsibility, contains the idea that body and heart/mind are interdependent: what happens to one affects the other. There is a principle of inter-being within us, as well as between us and other beings. So we must ask how our work affects our bodies and souls. If our spirits are crushed, our bodies will suffer; if our bodies are harmed, our souls will feel diminished. As we write, this area of Ontario is in the grip of a SARS crisis (a severe and infectious form of atypical pneumonia), and healthcare workers are being put under enormous stress. They want to do their jobs and care for the sick, but are at risk themselves of contracting the virus and falling ill. Part of their suffering comes from the feeling that they are not adequately valued and protected, and so the crisis is taking its toll on their spirits as well as their physical health.

Cultivating responsibility means understanding that we are inter-connected in body, mind and spirit, as well as with all living beings. It also means acknowledging that the other is a person too, not just an object. "When we are approached casually or carelessly," writes Thich Nhat Hanh, "we feel insulted in our body and soul" [Nhat Hanh 1995, 97]. We feel used, unheard, depersonalized. This is true in our relationships at work as well as in our intimate relationships. A disrespectful boss who treats employees with disdain or hostility violates their personhood — and sacrifices their respect. Management that is concerned about profit more than people is not acting with commitment and responsibility, the hallmarks of this precept. The resulting hurt and resentment take their toll on the mood at the workplace, on the individuals there, and on the output of the work. Everything is inter-connected: everything "inter-is."

The fourth precept traditionally prohibited telling lies, exaggerating, speaking with a "forked tongue," and using foul language. Thich Nhat Hanh sees it in essence as teaching loving, truthful speech and deep listening, in order to create trust, harmony, and reconciliation. It is a teaching about communication. "Never in the history of humankind have we had so many means of communication," he writes, "yet we remain islands" [Nhat Hanh 1995, 102]. The Buddhist practice of mindful speech trains a person to refrain from speaking impulsively, untruthfully, or harshly, in ways that cause harm. It is the exact opposite of the brash "shooting from the lip" of much communication in the Western world. It also stands as a contrast to the manipulation of truth that we take almost for granted now — the spin-doctoring of political statements, the massaging of a business's finances, the twisting of truth in advertising.

In a story that is all too typical of our society's attitude to truth, Nhat Hanh describes a corporate director of communications who confided in him that he could not tell the truth about his company's products, or sales would fall. Instead, he was both lying about their good points and remaining silent about their potential harm. He felt trapped in the deceit.

Truthful speech can require enormous courage. "Whistle blow-ers" who speak out about the corruption or cover-ups in their workplaces are often treated harshly, not rewarded. But Buddhist teaching is clear: without mindful, truthful, loving speech, as well as a willingness to listen to the other and be open to a different perspective, the world will continue to be fragmented, violent, and full of unnecessary suffering.

The fifth precept relates to what we consume and what, in turn, we give out to the world. Nhat Hanh interprets this as promoting healthy nourishment of our bodies, minds, and souls in order for self-transformation and the healing of society to be possible. Once again, he relates it to the concept of inter-being: "When you are able to get out of the shell of your small self," he says, "you will see that you are interrelated to everyone and everything, that your every act is linked with the whole of humankind and the whole cosmos" [Nhat Hanh 1955, 106]. Individualism teaches that we are our own bosses: if we choose to drink, smoke, and overwork, for example, we believe we have a right to do so, as long as we are not harming others. But in Buddhist thought our actions *always* affect others. Great mindfulness is therefore needed, so that what we consume (from food and drink to ideas and possessions) does not create more suffering for us or the world.

This is a real challenge for a society built on mind*less* consumerism. Many who are on a cycle of ceaseless working and spending feel as though they are locked on a treadmill. The possibility of saying No to the consumerist orthodoxy seems unthinkable. But Buddhist wisdom teaches that with a change in thinking and behaviour, liberation from the traps of our own making is possible. "The energy we need," says Nhat

Hanh, "is not fear or anger, but understanding and compassion … gained by deep touching and deep listening in a daily life of prayer, contemplation, and meditation" [Nhat Hanh, 1995, 110, 112]. As one practises the Five Precepts, preferably with the support of others, it becomes possible to engage in the workaday world with a mindfulness that leads toward freedom and peace.

How to survive in dangerous times: Inspiration from the Tao Te Ching

The Tao Te Ching (Dao De Jing), or Book of the Way, was written some five hundred years before the time of Christ, and is thought to be a compilation of the teachings of an anonymous Chinese elder nicknamed The Old Master, or Lao-Tzu (Laozi). It is a manual for rulers and bureaucrats on the art of living in dangerous times, written in a culture and context of violence and instability. A present-day Canadian Taoist has called it advice for survival in "a managerial piranha tank." Poet Stephen Mitchell describes it more loftily as "radiant with humor and grace and large heartedness and deep wisdom: one of the wonders of the world" [Mitchell 1988, vii]. Like Buddhism, it emerged in a culture very different from our own, and many of its teachings run counter to the accepted thinking of our day. For that reason it can jolt us out of habits of thought, and open a new way of seeing the world and living in it.

At the heart of the Tao is the concept of arriving after intense struggle at a place of not-doing, or surrender to the flow and inevitability of the universe. This is often misunderstood as passivity or fatalism, and seems at odds with a work ethic, for example, that stresses the importance of striving to accomplish things, make things happen, and be a success. But, explains Mitchell, the truth is that when we enter fully into the wisdom of the universe and trust it, action becomes effortless and natural: "The game plays the game; the poem writes the poem; we can't tell the dancer from the dance" [viii]. This is in fact akin to the modern concept of "flow" in work — the recognition that forcing inspiration or harmony or excellent work is impossible: rather, we must set up the right conditions and then get out of the way and let the process unfold naturally.

The Tao Te Ching is enjoying a rediscovery in our day, and is being read with twenty-first century eyes for its insights into leadership. It offers a wisdom that is counter to much that is mainstream in our culture, and is therefore a necessary counterpoint or balance. Consider the following extracts, and their relevance to the workplace.

Know contentment
And you will suffer no disgrace;
Know when to stop
And you will meet with no danger.
You can then endure
[Tao Te Ching, tr. D.C. Lau 1963, XLIV, 100].

He who knows contentment is rich
[Tao, XXXIII, 75].

*There is no crime greater than having too many de-
sires;
There is no disaster greater than not being content;
There is no misfortune greater than being covetous*
[Tao, XLVI, 105].

Just to read these lines can bring an unclenching, a deep exha-
lation and letting go, as we give ourselves permission to stop
striving. We know intellectually that we cannot control the
universe (we can barely control ourselves), and that our best
plans can be disrupted by unforeseen events. Yet we so often
act as though all the strings are in our hands, or should be, or
could be. We worry about what we are accomplishing, what
others think of us, what might happen if we relax our control.
The Tao, like other spiritual teachings, sets a wider perspective
before us, and invites us to stop gripping the steering wheel.
In Stephen Mitchell's words, inspired by the Tao:

*In dwelling, live close to the ground. In thinking, keep
to the simple.*

*In conflict, be fair and generous. In governing, don't try
to control.*

*In work, do what you enjoy. In family life, be
completely present* [ch. 8].

*Do your work, then step back. The only path to
serenity* [ch. 9].

He who clings to his work will create nothing that
endures.

If you want to accord with the Tao, just do your job,
then let go [ch. 24].

There is a simplicity about the wisdom of the Tao that encourages us not to take ourselves so seriously. It is reminiscent of Jesus' teachings about not worrying, where he pointed out that all our anxiety cannot add an hour longer to our lives, or an inch more to our height. Instead, he invited his followers to consider "the lilies of the field," gloriously beautiful and utterly free from striving. They were to be the symbol of deep trust [Matthew 6:25f]. Letting go of the anxious desire to control is key to being truly present to our world and our work. And, paradoxically, as we slowly and painfully learn to surrender and trust, like a swimmer entrusting her body to be held up by the water, so we discover that we can swim far more effectively than when we thrashed around.

To suggest to the Western culture of work that we need to let go of our desire for success is heresy: with all its accompanying images of wealth, status, and power, success is at the heart of the American dream. Yet the Tao and other spiritual teachings from many traditions know that when we pin our self-esteem and life energy onto the hope for success, we become ungrounded and prey to inflated ideas of our own importance, or illusory feelings of our worthlessness. Instead, we can gradually learn to take our successes with a pinch of salt when they come, and our failures as learnings. Neither one needs to be given ultimate value.

Fame or integrity: which is more important?
Money or happiness: which is more valuable?
Success or failure: which is more destructive?...
Be content with what you have; rejoice in the way
 things are.
When you realize there is nothing lacking,
the whole world belongs to you
[Mitchell 1988, ch. 44].

Paradox is at the heart of the Tao: like Zen koans (riddles or problems) and like the parables of Jesus that turned accepted wisdom on its head, these teachings ask us to reconsider what we assume to be true. Is more money really what we want? Is success really going to be the making of us? Is our work really the most important thing? "Don't try to 'figure out' paradoxes," advises author William Martin, in his book relating the Tao Te Ching to Christian pastoring. "Live with them and let their seeming non-rationality quiet down the overactive synapses of your beleaguered left brain" [Martin 1994, 22]. The Taoist path leads us away from the world of control to a place of surrender; from logic to paradox; from striving to serenity. And work can then flow as naturally as water through a channel.

Holy work and holy rest: Jewish approaches to work and Sabbath

There is a linguistic link in Hebrew between work and worship: the word "avodah" means both worship of God, and work or service. Unlike the Greek word for work, which is related to the word for pain or punishment, the Hebrew language makes an implicit connection between the holiness of what we do in the world, and the holiness of what we do in sacred times and spaces. Both work and worship can honour God and be holy acts. The Genesis text about Adam's curse, which became so central to a Christian ethic of working by the sweat of one's brow, did not develop in the same way in Judaism. Work could be hard, but it was holy and to be loved, not endured.

You shall eat the fruit of the labour of your hands;
you shall be happy, and it shall go well with you
[Psalm 128:2].

"Love work," says Shemaiah, one of the fathers of the Jewish Mishnah tradition. And another teacher of that tradition, Rabbi Nathan, explains this by saying: "This teaches that one should love work and that no one should hate it. For even as the Torah was given as a covenant, so was work given as a covenant; as it is said, 'Six days you shall labour and do all your work; but the seventh day is a day of rest unto the Eternal your God' "[Exodus 20:9] [Avot de-Rabbi Natan 11:1]. The focus is on the commandment to work and rest, both being understood as part of God's gracious covenant with humanity.

Work in this light is even regarded as essential for right spiritual development. There is a suspicion that religious activity alone, for example, can lead one astray. Rabban Gamaliel said, "Study of Torah [the body of Jewish religious and ethical teachings] combined with an occupation is good, for labour at both keep sin out of one's mind. But study of Torah alone, without an occupation, will in the end come to naught, and even on occasion sin" [Pirkei Avot 2:2]. Similarly, a total lack of work is considered dangerous: "If someone has no work to do, what should that person do? If there is a run down yard or field, let that person go and occupy himself with it…. One dies only out of idleness" [Avot de-Rabbi Natan 11:1].

The balance for work in Judaism is not idleness but Sabbath — a day of rest for all levels of society, and a day that comes every week, not once in a while. Rabbi Heschel writes, "The Sabbath is not for the sake of the weekdays; the weekdays are for the sake of the Sabbath. It is not an interlude but the climax of living…. Call the Sabbath a delight: a delight to the soul and a delight to the body" [Heschel 1951, 14,18]. In contrast again to some Christian traditions that made Sunday a cheerless, highly restrictive day of forced inactivity and religious observance, the Jewish tradition emphasizes the joyfulness of Sabbath, which is to be a feast for the body and soul. It is a day that revolves around family and prayer, food and celebration, study of the Torah and repose. It re-creates life in the Garden of Eden.

In our day, when the pace of life and work is so unremitting, a rediscovery of Sabbath principles is badly needed. We no longer have a day when workplaces do not open: it is business as usual, 24/7, unless we create pauses. Sabbath is about intentionally stopping, letting go of work and remembering to relax and leave things to God for a day. As Heschel says, "The world has already been created and will survive without the help of [humanity]" [Heschel 1951, 13]. Sabbath is about being instead of doing, giving thanks instead of worrying, praising instead of petitioning. In Matthew Fox's words, "The seventh day is created all over again when we celebrate Sabbath. The holy play of Sabbath preceded creation and completes creation.... The seventh day marked a very special creation: that of *Menuha* or happiness, stillness, peace, and harmony, of tranquility, serenity, and repose. Divine repose is at the heart of Sabbath; we can all participate in it, and in so doing we taste 'eternal life' " [Fox 1995, 271].

The commandment regarding the Sabbath begins with the key word, *Remember:* "Remember the Sabbath day, and keep it holy." It is as though we are likely to forget. The demands of life, whether as a wandering tribe of nomads in a hostile, barren desert, or a driven generation of professionals in a competitive, capitalist society, draw us into anxiety, greed, possessiveness and selfishness. The children of Israel, in the stories of their time in the wilderness, repeatedly fell into grumbling about how hard life was, and even suggested that slavery might be preferable [see Exodus 16]. They were provided with food, then tried to hoard it. They bickered among themselves and kicked against Moses, their leader. How very contemporary they sound! And in the midst of this turmoil comes the command to remember the Sabbath and keep it holy. The Sabbath calls us back to ourselves, to our origins, to a simple dependence on God's grace.

And the Sabbath is deeply egalitarian, not meant only for an élite leisured class. It is meant as a day of rest for all: "You shall not do any work — you, your son or your daughter, your male or female slave ... or the alien resident in your towns" [Exodus 20:10]. More than that, it extends to all working beasts, too: "Your ox or your donkey, or any of your livestock" [Deuteronomy 5:14]. The vision is of a society that cyclically and holistically is rejuvenated. There is to be no exhausting of the energy of any creature. One day a week, all beings are equal as they return to Eden. Like the Jewish concept of the Jubilee, the fiftieth year when debts are to be released and wealth redistributed in Israel [see Leviticus 25], the Sabbath is, to use Fox's term, "a safety valve" for the misuse of power and money. It recalls us to a sense of justice, and to God.

There is a wisdom about the Sabbath practice that goes beyond merely resting or worshipping: with a balance of holy work and holy rest we have a chance of relearning what our lives are really for and discovering a rhythm of action and reflection that the whole world badly needs, if it is to be saved from depleting itself catastrophically. "Without stopping the work we are doing," observes Fox, "it is unlikely that we will be able to address the work that needs doing. This stopping, this ability to let go and let be, is a spiritual act. In Buddhism, it is called non-action; [medieval mystic] Eckhart called it letting go; [St.] Paul called it emptying. The Jewish tradition called it Shabbat. Today we might all call it common sense. Or survival. We will do it together or we will perish together" [Fox 1995, 274].

The yoga of work: Hindu teachings from the Bhagavad Gita

Hinduism is associated with an enormous body of literature, rather than one single book equivalent to the Bible. The Bhagavad Gita is one poem, and is part of the Mahabharata collection of writings. On the surface, it recounts a dialogue between Arjuna, a reluctant warrior, and Krishna, a god-incarnation. Metaphorically, it teaches about how to engage in the battle between wisdom and ignorance, light and darkness, within us. In the introduction to his translation of the Bhagavad Gita from its original Sanskrit, Juan Mascaró writes, "A spiritual reader of the *Gita* will find in it the great spiritual struggle of a human soul" [Mascaró, tr. 1962, 23]. It speaks of the human fear of death and destruction, and the desire for peace. It is a call to action in the world, but action with detachment, with a self-offering to God. It explains what holy work or action is, and how every human being, no matter of what station in life, can practise this sort of work.

Like other spiritual classics, the Gita's words ring true down the centuries and across cultures:

What is work? What is beyond work? ... I will teach thee the truth of pure work, and this truth shall make thee free.
Know therefore what is work, and also know what is wrong work....
He whose undertakings are free from anxious desire and fanciful thought, whose work is made pure in the fire of wisdom: he is called wise by those who see.
In whatever work he does such a man in truth has peace: he expects nothing, he relies on nothing, and ever has fullness of joy.
He has no vain hopes, he is the master of his soul, he surrenders all he has, only his body works: he is free from sin.

He is glad with whatever God has given him, and he
has risen above the two contraries here below; he is
without jealousy, and in success or in failure he is one:
his works bind him not.
... his mind has found peace in wisdom, and his work
is a holy sacrifice. The work of such a man is pure.
Who in all his work sees God, he in truth goes unto
God: God is his worship [4.16–24].

These are themes found in many spiritual teachings around the world: gratitude, detachment from outcomes, cessation of anxiety, a focus on God rather than on success. In Hinduism this is the "yoga of holy work." Yoga here does not mean the physical stretches and poses that we are familiar with in the West, but is a word meaning at root "union" or "yoke" — that which joins us to God in inner communion and love. "Whatever you do," says the Gita, "or eat, or give, or offer in adoration, let it be an offering to me" [9.27].

With this perspective, even the most lowly, servile work can become a means to draw close to God and bring joy. Mascaró explains: "All life is action, but every little finite action should be a surrender to the Infinite, even as breathing in seems to be the receiving of the gift of life, and the breathing out a surrender into the infinite Life. Every little work in life, however humble, can become an act of creation and therefore a means of salvation... When vision is pure and when creation is pure there is always joy" [Mascaró, tr. 1962, 32]. From priestly work to manual labour, right across the caste system of ancient India, to the boardrooms, factories, hospitals, and kitchens of our society, one can make work an act of worship as an offering to God. And no work done in that spirit is impure or unacceptable.

The Gita teaches that as we come to know that the Spirit dwelling in a human body is part of the supreme God, so we can escape the feeling that we are being swept along blindly through life:

> *The Spirit ... watches, gives blessing, bears all, feels all.*
> *He is called the Lord Supreme....*
> *He who knows in truth this Spirit and knows nature*
> *with its changing conditions, wherever this man may*
> *be he is no more whirled round by fate [or rebirth].*
> *Some by the Yoga of meditation, and by the grace of*
> *the Spirit, see the Spirit in themselves; some [see it] by*
> *the Yoga of the vision of Truth; and others by the Yoga*
> *of work* [3.22 –24].

Life is hard and uncertain: we are not in control of circumstances, and times will inevitably come when we suffer. But our focus is everything. Eastern traditions teach meditative practices that train the mind to stay focused on the Infinite, the body to rest in stillness, and the soul to let go of ego desires:

> *This man of harmony surrenders the reward of his*
> *work and thus attains final peace....*

The ruler of his soul surrenders in mind all work, and rests in the joy of quietness in the castle of the nine gates of his body: he neither does selfish work nor causes others to do it [5.12,13].

This man sees and has no doubts: he surrenders, he is pure and has peace.Work, pleasant or painful, is for him joy.
For there is no man on earth who can fully renounce living work, but he who renounces the reward of his work is in truth a man of renunciation.
When work is done for a reward, the work brings pleasure, or pain, or both, in its time; but when a man does work in Eternity, then Eternity is his reward [18.10–12].

There is a gentleness to the Gita: it does not demand extreme self-denial or condemn those who fall short of the ideal. "One should not abandon one's work, even if one cannot achieve it in full perfection; because every endeavour has some inherent imperfection, just as in all fire there is smoke" [18.48]. There is an acceptance that imperfection is part of our lives here on earth, and a quiet invitation to continue to walk toward the light, knowing that "God dwells in the heart of all beings … thy God dwells in thy heart" [18.61].

Work and well-being: The Islamic message of balance

In his comprehensive book *The Religion of Islam* [1936, rev. 1990], Maulana Muhammad Ali writes that "Islam places great emphasis on the necessity for hard work and the dignity of labour" [584]. Right belief and good works together are the marks of a true Muslim. And he describes the Prophet Muhammad himself as "an indefatigable worker ... praying to God [by night] ... doing every kind of work in the day time. No work was too low for him. He would milk his own goats, patch his own clothes and mend his own shoes. In person he would dust his home and assist his wife in her household duties. In person he would do shopping, not only for his own household but also for his neighbours and friends. He worked like a labourer in the construction of the mosque.... He never despised any work, however humble, notwithstanding the dignity of his position as Prophet, as generalissimo and as king" [Ali 1990, 584–585].

Work in Islam is not pursued for wealth, status or power for their own sake. Neither is it seen as a chore, a curse, or a necessary safeguard against sin. Instead, work is intended to bring well-being to both the individual and society. Work of any kind, if done ethically and well, is part of a Muslim's life of faith and contributes to the betterment of the world. The yardstick for work is that it should promote economic well-being for all, universal justice, and equity. "God desires ease for you," says the Qur'an (Koran), "and desires not hardship for you" [2:185]. And again, "God desires not to place a burden on you but He wishes to purify you and to complete His favour on you so that you may be grateful" [5:6].

There is no tension between the sacred and the secular in Islamic thought, or between the spiritual and the worldly. It is said that "the best of Muslims is [the one] who is concerned about the affairs of this world as well as the affairs of the Hereafter" [Ibn Majah, v. 2, 725:2143]. In Islam "the spiritual and the material have been so firmly dovetailed with each other that they may serve as a source of mutual strength and together contribute to real human welfare. The neglect of any one of these two aspects of life cannot lead [hu]mankind to true welfare" [Khurshid Ahmad 1976, 178]. Similarly, the Prophet Muhammad declared that the whole world was his prayer carpet or mosque: he had no need to separate his life of prayer and worship from his daily life.

This fundamental uniting of secular and spiritual has several important repercussions for the world of work. First, Muslims take time *in the midst* of their work to say their daily prayers. "Islam regards every place — whether it is one's dwelling place, the back of an animal, the board of a vessel on the surface of the sea, or a mosque specifically built for worship — as pure enough for the performance of worship" [Ahmad 1976, 111]. By extension, a factory, office building, school or any other workplace becomes a place of worship when a Muslim pauses to pray in accordance with the religious practice of Islam. Hammudah Abdalati writes that "the Muslim, by observing these prayers, marks the whole day with a spiritual stamp in the beginning, at the end and throughout.... Religion presents itself to all fields of activity. It becomes effective in shops and offices, homes and farms, factories and plants. It extends its light to every circle of business and work" [Abdalati 1978, 66–67].

In practical terms this has meant that Muslims at work request places where they may perform the required ablutions before praying, and rooms where their prayer mats may be rolled out and used. As employers accommodate these requests, the issue of spirituality at work becomes real and visible. And, paradoxically, as Muslims forge the way for these accommodations in Western workplaces, practitioners of other faiths are beginning to follow suit, taking time in their workday to pray or meditate.

A second result of the interweaving of the spiritual and the worldly is the strong insistence in Islam of right ethics at work. "Woe to those who deal in fraud," warns the Qur'an [83:1]. The devout life is one where employers deal fairly with their employees, and workers give of their best in return. Reasonable wages (with a minimum livable wage) are to be paid to all, and there must be no exploitation of another's need, no harsh working conditions or overwork, and no unfair remuneration. Begging by those who are able but unwilling to work is prohibited, and all who work must do so honestly, conscientiously, and efficiently. As for the social status and economic wealth acquired by those who work, all should have equal opportunities to advance and acquire material goods, and disparities of wealth between employers and employees are to be minimized.

Islam's vision of justice and equity for all underpins its work ethics. There is a rejection of the greedy individualism of capitalism, as well as resistance to the forms of socialism that sacrifice the needs and freedoms of the individual for the sake of the community. The goal is balance — balance between body and soul, the individual and the community, the material and the spiritual, socialism and capitalism, this world and the hereafter. For the well-being of all, both individually and collectively, there must be an equilibrium that reconciles opposites by allowing each some scope, in moderation.

"God loves not those who exceed the limits," says the Qur'an [5:87]. The world and its pleasures are to be enjoyed: Islam is not an ascetic, self-denying religion. But balance and moderation are key to human well-being. Work, then, is approached in the same light: a moderate, ethical day's work, infused with prayer and rewarded with a reasonable wage, brings approval from God, satisfaction for the individual, and greater well-being for the world.

CHAPTER 9

How to Get Started

1. Prayers for the Workplace

On the way to work:

God be in my work today,
God be in my mind today,
God be in my heart today,
God be in my midst today.
Amen.

For all who work:

God who labours with us,
may we work with spirit,
live with love,
and be at peace.

Let our work be the place
where our gifts
meet the world's needs,
that all may be blessed.
Amen.

Before a difficult meeting:
O God,
give me courage to speak my truth,
openness to listen to others,
patience for the journey ahead
and wisdom to find your path.
Amen.

When anxious and tired:
Teach me, Holy One, how to let go.
Receive my work as I surrender it to you.
My life is small and my perspective limited:
let me trust all things
to your greater vision.
Show me how to be
in this moment
at peace,
and to leave the rest to you.
Amen.

At the end of the work day:

May all my work be blessed by you,
May those I met be touched by you,
May all I did be done for you,
May this day's end be rest in you.
Amen.

2. A Breath Prayer

This can be done at any time during the day, when you want to de-stress, refocus on God, and come back to a centre of peacefulness. It is part of the ancient tradition known as practising the presence of God.

Stop what you're doing, breathe slowly in and out, and relax your body. Bring your awareness and attention to the next few breaths, focusing with as much concentration as you can on the sensation of the breath entering your body and then leaving it. If your mind wants to dodge away or comment or juggle other thoughts, just bring it gently back to watching the breath.

Once your breath has become even and regular, slightly deeper than normal but without strain, bring a simple phrase to mind to connect yourself to God as you breathe. For example, mentally say on the in-breath, "Holy Spirit," and on the out-breath, "fill me." Or "O God, grant me peace," or "For you, O Christ." Choose words that express what your deepest desire is in that moment, as simply as you can. Repeat the phrase slowly and silently as you continue to breathe in and out. Each time the mind wanders, bring it gently back to the breathing and the words.

When you are ready to return to what you were doing (or if you are interrupted and have to return quickly), continue to keep part of your mind aware of your breathing. You may find that the phrase continues to run through your head. This sort of breath prayer can become an anchor to hold onto when life around you is like a turbulent sea. Writing the phrase out and placing it where you can easily see it at work can also help you stay connected to the still point where God is.

3. Knowing Yourself

Much of the spiritual journey is a quest for deeper self-knowledge. From this place of *being* comes a sense of what is congruent in terms of *doing*. The more you know yourself honestly and realistically, the more likely you are to be able to choose work that uses your gifts and does not try to squash a round peg into a square hole. As Parker Palmer writes in his wise little book, *Let Your Life Speak*, "If we are unfaithful to true self, we will make promises we cannot keep, build houses from flimsy stuff, conjure dreams that devolve into nightmares, and other people will suffer" [Palmer 2000, 31].

Certain tools can be helpful in this process of finding "true self." You may wish to delve into one or more of the popular personality type systems. These are based primarily on the psychological research of Carl Jung, who lived from 1875 to 1961. His work is published in *Psychological Types* [1981]. Isabel

Briggs Myers and her daughter Kathryn Cook Briggs were the first to develop a personality types inventory, known as the Myers-Briggs Type Indicator (MBTI) instrument. The MBTI, based on sixteen personality types, is still very popular, and there are many trained career and personal counsellors who can administer and interpret the results for you.

There are many popular systems based on Jung's theory: David Keirsey's "Temperament Sorter" [*Please Understand Me II: Temperament, Character, Intelligence*]; "True Colors," developed by Don Lowry [*True Colors: Building Esteem with Your Family*]; "Heroic Archetypes" by Carol S. Pearson [*The Hero Within: Six Archetypes We Live By*], and a recent one called "Personality Dimensions" by Lynda McKim and Robert McKim [*Personality Dimensions*]. Some systems are also available online.

With all of the type and temperament systems, the goal is to understand ourselves better so that we can relate to each other in positive ways, and find work that matches our gifts and characteristics. It can be very helpful for a work team to be guided through one of these systems so that they can understand each member of the team better in order to improve communications, interactions, and spirituality at work.

4. Personal Mission Statement

A personal mission statement can serve as a guide to your spiritual journey. When you are faced with choices, your personal mission statement can help remind you of what you hold most dear. Your mission statement should inspire you!

"To thine own self be true," by Shakespeare [*Hamlet*, act 1, scene iii, line 78], could be considered a personal mission statement. Two popular books — *First Things First* by Stephen Covey et al. [1994] and *The Path: Creating Your Mission Statement for Work and for Life* by Laurie Beth Jones [1996] describe personal mission statements as self-assessment/reflection tools to help individuals with career planning and day-to-day decision- making. A personal mission statement may even assist in discerning your calling.

Mission statements have been used by organizations for years. Businesses try to keep their mission statements brief and "catchy" so that they will be remembered by customers and can be used in advertising, e.g., GE's "We bring good things to life" and Acura's: "Designed with purpose. Driven by passion." Covey et al. [1994, 113] describe "empowering mission statements which represent the deepest and best within us." Their examples are typically a paragraph long.

Laurie Beth Jones advocates the use of personal mission statements in a single-sentence style, e.g., Jones's own mission statement is: "To recognize, promote and inspire the divine connection in myself and others" [Jones 1996, 222]. She outlines a four-step method to create a personal mission statement. The steps include: selecting action words that are personally meaningful (e.g., affirm, create, discover, motivate, and understand); indicating a personal principle, cause, value, or purpose; declaring a group or field that is the focus of your work (e.g., elderly people, families, children, the environment, education, and the performing arts); and finally, putting the three elements together [Jones 1996, 50–63]. Here are some examples developed using this technique by University of Guelph students in the Transition from School to Work course:

> *"To promote safety, well-being, and self-esteem for all children."*

> *"I will live each day with respect for myself and others, facing challenges as they come and learning from my mistakes in order to become a stronger person."*

> *"To cure the sick, alleviate the suffering, and inspire well-being amongst the people in my community."*

Please note that this technique does not work for everyone – try it and see if it is helpful. If not, then do some journalling and explore different ideas, or go for a walk in the woods or on a beach and let your mind wander! Also, personal mission statements are dynamic. As you change roles, jobs, and interests, you may wish to create a new personal mission statement.

5. Journalling Exercises

Keeping a diary or a notebook with ideas, lists, recipes, and so forth is a common practice. Journalling involves much more than writing in a diary or book of notes. Through journalling, you can meditate, pray, deal with problems, unlock creative ideas, write a poem or story, draw a picture, and document your spiritual journey. Many famous people have kept journals, including Leonardo de Vinci. Although any literate person can journal, there are techniques and exercises that can open up a whole new experience for you.

In her wonderful book on journalling, *Writing Down the Bones* [1986], Natalie Goldberg presents two "rules of journalling" that are particularly helpful:

1. *Date every entry, and*
2. *There are no other rules.*

Dating each entry is useful when you go back and read your journals. Thinking in terms of no other rules opens up journalling as a technique that can serve a myriad of purposes.

Journalling should not become an activity that you feel you need to do every day, like a diary. Journal whenever you wish — let it be an activity that opens up your spiritual world.

Journalling is a private activity. You need to feel confident that no one will read your journal without your permission. If you know that others may read your journal, you will edit as you write so as not to hurt that person's feelings. Discuss this with your life partner, children, and others so that they know that your journal is private. Leonardo de Vinci kept his journals private by writing in a code and backwards. Hopefully, you will not need to do that.

You might be able to start your journalling by attending a workshop. Workshops are typically related to creative writing, since many writers use journalling as a way develop their writing. Workshops will typically involve several exercises. Some examples follow. You may wish to start your journalling session with a meditation and/or prayer. Christina Baldwin's *Life's Companion: Journal Writing as a Spiritual Quest* [1990] contains excellent guidance on journalling as well as meditations. It helps to find a quiet place to journal. You may wish to find a special place where you journal. It might be nice to bring your journal to a coffee shop and write while you enjoy a tea or coffee.

Exercise 1. Flow-writing
Books on journalling, including Goldberg's [1986], suggest this as a great warm-up: Simply write in your journal without stopping and without lifting up your pen for ten minutes. If you can't think of anything to write, then write, "I can't think of anything to write. I can't think of anything to write." After a short while your brain will tire of this and out will flow your feelings. Ten minutes sounds like a long time until you try this exercise. Typically, when people check their watch, they find they have been writing for twenty or thirty minutes.

Exercise 2. Introduce yourself to your journal
Write an autobiography as a list of characteristics, a list of your different roles, as a story, or in any way that you like.

Exercise 3. Write a letter that you will not mail
Write to someone living or dead and tell him or her what you have always wanted to say but cannot. Be honest.

Exercise 4. Describe an object
Write about an object — a pinecone, spoon, candle, whatever — in great detail. Really see the object and write about it.

Exercise 5. Create a scenario

For example: You're walking through a dense forest. The path leads by a small opening to a cave. As you are passing the cave, a voice calls out, "Please help me!" from within the cave. What happens next?

Exercise 6. Your memorial service

Imagine that you arrive at a church. You enter and see a casket at the front of the church. You walk down the aisle and notice that the casket is open. You look in and see it's you. What will the people giving testimonials say? What memories will they share? What hymns will the choir sing in your honour? Another similar exercise is to write your own obituary.

Exercise 7. Dialogue

Create a conversation between you and Jesus, God, a deceased loved one, whoever you wish. Write both sides of the conversation. This can be a very powerful spiritual experience, a form of prayer.

When you are journalling, use as much detail as possible. This will help your writing and also help settle you into journalling. In workshops the group may debrief after each exercise — not necessarily reading what they have written, but discussing how well the exercise worked. You can do this on your own. Try out the exercises and decide which ones work well for you.

In terms of equipment, all you need is a journal and a pen. Bookshops now have a wide variety of journals (which must mean that lots of people are journalling) or you can buy a simple notebook. Free spirits tend to like pages without lines, others like the security of ruled lines — both types are available. Fountain pens are nice for writing in a journal but, of course, any style of pen that you like will work. You may wish to use different colours of inks.

6. The Examen: Finding God in Your Day

In the Ignatian tradition of Christian prayer there is a simple exercise that can be done at the end of the day to develop greater awareness of the presence of God in daily life. Called the *examen*, or examination of consciousness, this practice can teach us how to live and work increasingly in cooperation with the Spirit, and how to notice what draws us away from God. It also deepens our gratitude, helps us to notice moments of grace, and infuses life with meaning.

There are three basic steps to this practice:

1. *Relax*
At the end of the day, slow your pace, take some time to walk or sit quietly, maybe light a candle.

2. *Review*
Go over the day's events in your mind, and ask yourself (a) when you felt most alive, close to God, at home in the world, happy, or open-hearted, and (b) when you felt most drained, disconnected from God, out of sorts, unhappy, or closed off. You may find yourself recalling major incidences, or small moments. Both are significant.

3. *Reflect*

Either by yourself, with another, or with God, pay attention to those significant positive and negative feelings. Observe them gently, noticing without judging.

For example, you might have recalled that there was a moment in the day when someone criticized you and you felt angry, and another moment when you took a lunch break with a colleague and you felt your spirits lift. Don't replay angry thoughts about the person who criticized you, or fantasize about taking two-hour lunch breaks with this colleague every day! Just notice the anger and the lifted spirits, reflect on where they come from inside you, and be open to what both may have to teach you. In this example, you may become aware that criticism triggers old wounds from childhood that are yet to be healed. And you may realize that you need to nurture supportive friendships at work.

Over time, as you practise the examen and become more attentive to the daily movements within your heart, you can learn to live more closely connected to what brings you life and draws you closer to God. A difficult moment in the day may propel you into despair and loneliness, or may bring you closer in relationship with God. The examen raises to consciousness what happens in your inner life and invites you to make spiritual choices for change. Thus both good days and bad can be opportunities to understand the story of our own life better, and find the healing movement of God within it.

An excellent book on the examen is *Sleeping With Bread: Holding What Gives You Life* [Dennis Linn, Matthew Linn, and Sheila Fabricant Linn 1995].

7. How to Form a Spirituality in the Workplace Group

Our experience has been that people from a variety of faith backgrounds, from the practising to the lapsed to the agnostic, share a great interest in connecting their work with their spirituality. They may not use these terms; in fact, some would talk about purpose, meaning, values, direction, rather than spirituality. But there is a shared need for work to be about more than earning money, getting promotions, or making products, and for work to cohere with each one's deepest identity or soul.

Bringing such people together is the single most useful thing to do. If a time, a topic, and a place can be regularly set aside, the people and conversations will follow. We might almost dare to say, "Schedule it, and they will come!"

Of course, a sense that this is a safe place to talk honestly and openly, as human beings rather than as hierarchically ranked workers, needs to be created. It is possible to have a successful spirituality in the workplace group within a company or institution with participants from all levels of the hierarchy, if basic ground rules are accepted. These might include the following:

1. All participants are of equal value.
2. All contributions are respected and received non-judgementally.
3. Conversations are not debates, arguments, or policy-making occasions.
4. Respectful listening to one another is essential.

5. *The group is confidential.*

6. *Proselytizing of any kind is not acceptable.*

A simple focus for regular meetings is to discuss an agreed upon book. A great number of books exist on the theme of spirituality at work, so it need not be difficult to find a suitable one.

The format for a weekly hour-long meeting might be:

Gathering

People arrive, settle in, and set the tone by lighting a candle, reading a prayer, or meditating for a few minutes together.

Check-in

Each person has the opportunity to reflect on the previous week, talking about any aspect of it that is significant. It is best if others listen rather than discuss, until all have had a chance to speak. Passing a "talking stick" object can be helpful: whoever has the talking stick may speak, and others listen until it is their turn to hold the stick. A playful way of doing the check-in and keeping it brief can be to ask for a summary statement in the form of a metaphor. For instance: "If you were the weather, what would you have been like this week?" Or, "If your life these days were like a landscape, what would it look like?"

Conversation

The group may choose to talk about any subject that came up during the check-in, or to focus on the theme or chapter of the day. Again, it is important for the tone to be respectful and attentive, especially in a context where the norm in the workplace, by contrast, is for conversation to be oppositional, competitive, or controlling.

Conclusion
For a group like this to be viable, there needs to be a clear end time so that people can know they will be back at work punctually. Carving out even an hour to meet before, during, or after work is no small achievement for most of us, and our sense that there is just not enough time often prevents us from doing anything more than the essential work in front of us.

In between
Email conversations and contributions are a useful way to keep people connected throughout the week, or when they are unable to attend group meetings.

Sometimes a well-chosen quote read in the middle of a difficult day can inspire, support, or encourage a person who might otherwise be feeling isolated and defeated.

As a sense of community develops among group members, so, too, they can "leaven the dough" of the institution or company. The culture of overwork and competitiveness is a dominant reality for many of us at work, but a spirituality group in the midst of it can be creatively transformative as we support each other in engaging our best and deepest selves in work, and find our vocation and our God in the midst of it.

8. Outline for a Spirituality at Work Retreat Day

For those who have been meeting in a small group, or for any who are interested in setting aside a longer period of time to consider spirituality at work, a retreat day during a weekend can be a refreshing and illuminating experience. The day can be directed by a retreat leader, or designed and led collaboratively by a group. What follows is one example of how the time might be spent.

Arrival and refreshments.

Gathering ritual
A talking stick circle might be held, in which participants are invited to say why they came and what they are hoping to gain.

Meditation time
A breath prayer, examen, or other meditative practice.

Questions to ponder
A time for solo and group reflection on core questions such as those given throughout this book. This can be done through individual journalling first, followed by small group conversation.

Walking meditation
A labyrinth walk is particularly helpful for allowing questions to become clearer and insights to emerge.

Lunch and free time

Yoga or body work of another form

Small group conversation
What is emerging, stirring, calling?

Guided meditation and journalling

Closing ritual
A time of thanksgiving for a gift received, prayer for a grace needed, or naming an intention for the future.

--- CHAPTER 10 ---
Suggested Reading

Baldwin, Christina. 1990. *Life's Companion: Journal Writing as a Spiritual Quest.* Toronto: Bantam Books.

Bolman, Lee G., and Terrence E. Deal. 2001. *Leading with Soul: An Uncommon Journey of Spirit – New & Revised.* San Francisco: Jossey-Bass, Inc.

Conger, Jay, and Associates. 1994. *Spirit at Work: Discovering the Spirituality in Leadership.* San Francisco: Jossey-Bass, Inc.

Covey, Stephen R., Roger A. Merrill, and Rebecca R. Merrill. 1990. *First Things First: To Live, To Love, To Learn, To Leave a Legacy.* New York: Simon & Schuster.

Edwards, Tilden. 1992. *Sabbath Time.* Nashville: Upper Room Books.

Foster, Richard. 1981. *Freedom of Simplicity.* London: SPCK.

Fox, Matthew. 1995. *The Reinvention of Work: A New Vision of Livelihood for Our Time.* San Francisco: Harper.

Goldberg, Natalie. 1986. *Writing Down the Bones: Freeing the Writer Within.* Boston: Shambhala.

Greenleaf, Robert K. 2002. *Servant Leadership: A Journey into the Nature of Legitimate Power and Greatness – 25th Anniversary Edition.* New York: Paulist Press.

Havel, Václav. 1986. *Living in Truth: 22 Essays Published on the Occasion of the Award of the Erasmus Prize to Václav Havel.* Edited by Jan Vladislav. London: Faber & Faber.

Jones, Laurie Beth. 1996. *The Path: Creating Your Mission Statement for Work and for Life.* New York: Hyperion.

Leddy, Mary Jo. 2002. *Radical Gratitude.* New York: Orbis Books.

Levoy, Gregg. 1997. *Callings: Finding and Following an Authentic Life.* New York: Three Rivers Press.

Linn, Dennis, Matthew Linn, and Sheila Fabricant Linn. 1995. *Sleeping With Bread: Holding What Gives You Life.* New York: Paulist Press.

MacKenzie, Gordon. 1998. *Orbiting the Giant Hairball.* New York: Viking Press.

Palmer, Parker. 2000. *Let Your Life Speak: Listening for the Voice of Vocation.* San Francisco: Jossey-Bass Inc.

Whyte, David. 1994. *The Heart Aroused: Poetry and the Preservation of Soul in Corporate America.* New York: Doubleday.

_____. *Crossing the Unknown Sea: Work as a Pilgrimage of Identity.* 2001. New York: Riverhead Books.

See also the website for the Centre for Spirituality at Work: *www.SpiritualityAtWork.org*

--- CHAPTER 11 ---
Works Cited

Abdalati, Hammudah. 1978. *Islam in Focus.* Salimiah, Kuwait: Islamic Federation of Student Organisations.

Adams, Scott. 1996. *Fugitive from the Cubicle Police.* Kansas City: Andrews and McMeel.

Ahmad, Khurshid, ed. 1976. *Islam: Its Message and Meaning.* Markfield, UK: Islamic Foundation Limited.

Ali, Maulana Muhammad. 1936, rev. 1990. *The Religion of Islam.* Columbus, Ohio: Ahmadiyya Anjuman Isha'at Islam (Lahore).

Avot de-Rabbi Natan. See Goldin, Judah, tr. 1958, rev. 1990. *The Fathers According to Rabbi Nathan.* New Haven: Yale University Press.

Baldwin, Christina. 1990. *Life's Companion: Journal Writing as a Spiritual Quest.* Toronto: Bantam Books.

Bibby, Reginald. 2002. *Restless Gods: The Renaissance of Religion in Canada.* Toronto: Stoddard Publishing Co.

Carmichael, Alexander. 1994. *Carmina Gadelica*. Vol. III. Hudson, NY: Lindisfarne Press.

Covey, Stephen R. 1990. *The Seven Habits of Highly Effective People: Restoring the Character Ethic.* New York: Simon and Schuster.

Covey, Stephen R., Roger A. Merrill, and Rebecca R. Merrill. 1994. *First Things First: To Live, To Love, To Learn, To Leave a Legacy.* New York: Simon and Schuster.

Duxbury, Linda, Chris Higgins, and Donna Coghill. 2003. *Voices of Canadians.* Ottawa: Ministry of Labour.

Foster, Richard. 1981. *Freedom of Simplicity.* London: Triangle/SPCK.

Fox, Matthew. 1995. *The Reinvention of Work: A New Vision of Livelihood for Our Time.* San Francisco: Harper.

_____, ed. 1983. *Meditations with Meister Eckhart.* Santa Fe, New Mexico: Bear and Co.

Goldberg, Natalie. 1986. *Writing Down the Bones: Freeing the Writer Within.* Boston: Shambhala.

Harpur, Tom. 2002. *Finding the Still Point: A Spiritual Response to Stress.* Kelowna, BC: Northstone Publishing.

Heschel, Abraham Joshua. 1951. *The Sabbath.* New York: Farrar, Straus and Giroux.

Ibn Majah, v. 2, 725:2143. See Ahmad, Khurshid, ed. 1976, *Islam: Its Message and Meaning.*

Jones, Laurie Beth. 1996. *The Path: Creating Your Mission Statement for Work and for Life.* New York: Hyperion.

Jung, C. G. 1921, rev. 1981. *Psychological Types*. New Jersey: Princeton University Press.

Keirsey, David. 1998. *Please Understand Me II: Temperament, Character, Intelligence*. Del Mar, CA: Prometheus Nemesis Book Co.

Lao Tzu. *Tao Te Ching*. Translated by Stephen Mitchell (see below) 1998.

Lau, D.C., tr. 1963. *Tao Te Ching*. Hammondsworth, Middlesex: Penguin Books.

Leddy, Mary Jo. 2002. *Radical Gratitude*. New York: Orbis Books.

Levertov, Denise. 1997. *The Sapphire and the Stream: Selected Poems on Religious Themes*. New York: New Directions Publishing.

Levoy, Gregg. 1997. *Callings: Finding and Following an Authentic Life*. New York: Three Rivers Press.

Lowry, Donald. 1990. *True Colors: Building Esteem with Your Family*. Corona, CA: True Colors Publishing.

MacKenzie, Gordon. 1998. *Orbiting the Giant Hairball*. New York: Viking Press.

Martin, William. 1994. *The Art of Pastoring: Contemplative Reflections*. Decatur, GA: CTS Press.

Mascaro, Juan, tr. 1962. *Bhagavad Gita*. London: Penguin Books.

Maslow, Abraham. 1954, rev. 1987 by Frager, Robert, and James Fadiman. *Motivation and Personality*. New York: Addison-Wesley Publishing Company.

McKim, Lynda, and Robert McKim. 2003. *Personality Dimensions*. Concord, ON: Career/LifeSkills Resources, Inc.

Mitchell, Stephen, tr. 1998. *Tao Te Ching: A New English Version*. New York: HarperCollins.

Nhat Hanh, Thich. 1995. *Living Buddha, Living Christ*. New York: Riverhead Books.

Palmer, Parker. 2000. *Let Your Life Speak*. San Francisco: Jossey-Bass Inc.

Pearson, Carol S. 1989. *The Hero Within: Six Archetypes We Live By*. San Francisco: Harper.

Pirkei Avot (quoting Rabban Gamaliel). See Goldin, Judah, 1957, rev. 1984, *The Living Talmud*. New York: New American Library.

Qu'ran. See Ali, Abdullah Yusuf, tr. 1989, rev. 1997. *The Holy Qu'ran*. Bettsville, Maryland: amana publications. See also Ali, Maulana Muhammad, tr. 1951, *The Holy Qu'ran*. Lahore, Pakistan: Ahmadiyyah Anjuman Isha'at Islam.

Weber, Max. 1905, rev. 1958. *The Protestant Ethic and the Spirit of Capitalism*. New York: Scribner's Press.

Whyte, David. 1994. *The Heart Aroused: Poetry and the Preservation of Soul in Corporate America*. New York: Doubleday.

_____. 2001. *Crossing the Unknown Sea: Work as a Pilgrimage of Identity*. New York: Riverhead Books.

The Authors

Lucy Reid is an Anglican priest working in campus ministry at the University of Guelph. She fills an ecumenical role as part of a multi-faith team. Her special interests include faith development, spirituality in the workplace, women's spirituality and bereavement counselling. Since 1994 Lucy has been coordinating groups of faculty and staff on campus for "Spirit At Work" weekly gatherings and retreats. Lucy is married to an Anglican priest and has three teenage children.

Fred Evers is a Professor of Sociology and Director of the Educational Research & Development Unit at the University of Guelph. He teaches courses on leadership, organizational analysis, research methods, and the transition from school to work for Guelph students in the last year of studies. His publications include journal articles, chapters in books, papers in conference proceedings, and the book: *The Bases of Competence: Skills for Lifelong Learning and Employability* by Fred Evers, James Rush, and Iris Berdrow (Jossey-Bass, Inc., Publishers, San Francisco, 1998). He is currently working with Phil Gardner on a book for students making the transition from university to work. Fred has worked as a volunteer with youth groups in the Anglican Diocese of Niagara. He is married and has two daughters.

Path Books
A LIGHT TO MY PATH

We hope that you have enjoyed reading this Path Book. For more information about Path Books, please visit our website at **www.pathbooks.com**. If you have comments or suggestions about Path Books, please write us at publisher@pathbooks.com.

Other Path Books

Practical Prayer: Making Space for God in Everyday Life by Anne Tanner. A richly textured presentation of the history, practices, and implications of Christian prayer and meditation to help people live a rewarding life in a stressful world.
1-55126-321-1 $18.95
Meditation CD: 1-55126-348-3 $18.95
Audio cassette: 1-55126-349-1 $16.95
Leader's Guide: 1-55126-347-5 $18.95

Oceans of Grief and Healing Waters: A Story of Loss and Recovery by Marian Jean Haggerty. With courageous candour and strength, Marian Haggerty tells the story of her journey toward healing from grief, after the death of a loved one. This book can be a wonderful companion for those who are alone and grieving, helping them to understand that they do not journey by themselves.
1-55126-396-3 $16.95

Struggling with Forgiveness: Stories from People and Communities by David Self. These powerful firsthand stories reflect the tremendous range of our experience of conflict and forgiveness: in families, at work, between individuals, within whole societies. They reveal how forgiveness can break the cycle of bitterness, revenge, and violence. There is such possibility for release and healing.
ISBN 1-55126-395-5 $19.95

God with Us: The Companionship of Jesus in the Challenges of Life by Herbert O'Driscoll. In thirty-three perceptive meditations, Herbert O'Driscoll considers the challenges of being human, searches key events in the life of Jesus, and discovers new vitality and guidance for our living. He shows us how the healing wisdom and power of Jesus' life can transform our own lives today.
1-55126-359-9 $18.95

Canadian Church Diary
Specially designed for convenient note-taking and appointment-keeping, these diaries feature the liturgical calendars of the Christian year. Published annually. Please inquire.
Pocket $14.95 and Desk $19.95

Available from your local bookstore or
Anglican Book Centre, phone 1-800-268-1168
or write 80 Hayden Street, Toronto, ON M4Y 3G2